Para Julio y Cecili
con un abrazo cordial.

Jim

THE POET
IN PERU

LIVERPOOL MONOGRAPHS IN HISPANIC STUDIES

1

THE POET IN PERU

JAMES HIGGINS

ALIENATION AND THE QUEST FOR A SUPER-REALITY

X

FRANCIS CAIRNS

© 1982 James Higgins

Published by Francis Cairns
    The University, P.O. Box 147, Liverpool L69 3BX, Great Britain

First published 1982, as Volume 1 of the series *Liverpool Monographs in Hispanic Studies* (ISSN 0261-1538)

ISBN 0 905205 10 3

Printed in Great Britain by Redwood Burn Ltd., Trowbridge, Wiltshire.

CONTENTS

PART ONE : POETRY OF ALIENATION

1	José María Eguren	1
2	César Vallejo	24
3	Carlos Germán Belli	46
4	Antonio Cisneros	65

PART TWO : VISIONARY POETRY

1	José María Eguren	91
2	César Vallejo	109
3	César Moro	123
4	Martín Adán	145

FOREWORD

This book does not pretend to be a history of Peruvian poetry of this century. It is simply a study of six poets who stand out among their compatriots because of the quality and significance of their work, and of the manifestation in Peru of two tendencies of contemporary Western poetry. Not included are other equally important currents and many other estimable poets. It is truly remarkable that Peru should have produced so much excellent poetry in spite of adverse cultural conditions. I hope that this book will stimulate other scholars to pay due attention to the poets and poetic currents I have not been able to include.

Of the poets studied here only Vallejo has won true international fame. The others remain relatively unknown outside Peru, except among specialists, and there are few critical works devoted to them. Hence one of the objects of this book is to serve as introduction to the work of these poets who deserve to be better known.

With regard to the currents examined, the book lays no claim to originality since it deals with tendencies well known in the contemporary poetry of other countries. In studying their manifestation in Peru, I have sought to show the existence of certain literary traditions in the poetry of that country and to situate apparently very different poets within the context of those traditions. The first part, *Poetry of Alienation*, studies the various forms that the experience of alienation takes in the work of Eguren, Vallejo, Belli and Cisneros. The second part, *Visionary Poetry*, examines through the work of Eguren, Vallejo, Moro and Adán the concept of poetry as a vehicle for apprehending a greater reality. One of my main problems has been to find a suitable terminology. Hence I should point out that I use the word "alienation" in its widest sense and that I have opted for the term "visionary or neo-mystical poetry" for lack of a better one.

In the first part of the book my main concern has been to highlight that alienation as a widespread phenomenon common to many

Peruvian poets yet experienced in different ways by different individuals. I have preferred to avoid offering generalised and simplistic explanations of the causes of that phenomenon. It is clear that up to a point the experience of Peruvian artists merely reflects the general sense of frustration and disenchantment that is a feature of the modern Western world. It is equally clear, however, that their alienation also has its roots in the national situation of an underdeveloped country of the Third World. Even in the twentieth century Peru bears the mark of its colonial heritage in the persistence of antiquated social and political structures, centuries-old social injustices and economic backwardness and dependency, and far from producing a radical transformation of that society, a gradual and limited process of industrialisation has aggravated existing problems and tensions and created new ones. Furthermore, the cultural backwardness of a country with a high rate of illiteracy and a small reading public condemns the writer to a marginal role in society.

Eguren and Vallejo are allotted two chapters apiece and are included in both parts of the book. This not only highlights their stature and the difficulty of reducing their work to a single category, but is intended to demonstrate that the visionary poetics is a response to the experience of alienation. That experience is also implicitly present in the poetry of Moro and Adán.

Finally, I wish to express my gratitude to Carlos Germán Belli, Julio Ortega, Edmundo Bendezú and John Kinsella for the help they gave me in the preparation of different chapters. To them the book is dedicated.

James Higgins,
School of Hispanic Studies,
University of Liverpool.

PART ONE
POETRY OF ALIENATION

1

JOSE MARIA EGUREN

"No me encuentro en mi salsa,"[1] complains Carlos Germán Belli; "de paso estoy en una patria que nunca será mía,"[2] writes Wáshington Delgado in a book entitled *Destierro por vida*. Belli and Delgado, poets of the so-called generation of the fifties, express here a sense of alienation which is perhaps the most characteristic note of Peruvian poetry in this century, as, indeed, of all contemporary Western literature. The major Peruvian poets are outsiders who feel themselves out of place in the country and in the world where it has been their lot to live. Yet if theirs has been a painful experience in personal terms, it has been fruitful for poetry. For not only has their disconformity with their world impelled them to write and furnished them with poetic material, but the best of them have embraced their estrangement and have used their isolation to develop a style of their own.

An exemplary case is that of José María Eguren (1874-1942), who turned his back on society to lead a secluded life in the tranquil little seaside resort of Barranco outside Lima. His vital attitude is defined in "Peregrín cazador de figuras", a kind of "portrait of the artist", where he presents himself in the guise of Peregrín, who, from a lonely *mirador*, peers into the night and explores a dark, mysterious landscape which is a symbol of the world of the imagination:[3]

En el mirador de la fantasía,
al brillar del perfume
tembloroso de armonía;
en la noche que llamas consume;
cuando duerme el ánade implume,
los órficos insectos se abruman

1. Carlos Germán Belli, *El pie sobre el cuello* (Montevideo: Alfa, 1967), p.16.
2. Wáshington Delgado, *Un mundo dividido* (Lima: Casa de la Cultura del Perú, 1970), p.208.
3. J.M. Eguren, *Obras completas* (Lima: Mosca Azul Editores, 1974), p.74. All references are to this edition. Eguren published three volumes of poetry: *Simbólicas* (1911), *La canción de las figuras* (1916) and *Poesías* (1929); this last book includes the collections *Sombra* and *Rondinelas*. He also wrote essays in prose which were published by Estuardo Núñez in 1959 under the title *Motivos estéticos*.

> y luciérnagas fuman;
> cuando lucen los silfos galones, entorcho,
> y vuelan mariposas de corcho
> o los rubios vampiros cecean,
> o las firmes jorobas campean,
> por la noche de los matices,
> de ojos muertos y largas narices;
> en el mirador distante,
> por las llanuras;
> Peregrín cazador de figuras,
> con ojos de diamante
> mira desde las ciegas alturas.

It is only after a long enumeration that we are actually introduced to Peregrín in his solitary vigil. In this way the structure of the poem conveys a sense of isolation, an impression that is reinforced by the nocturnal setting and by the references to the remoteness and loftiness of the *mirador*. Thus Peregrín appears as a completely isolated figure engaged in an essentially solitary activity. Through him Eguren expresses his lack of sympathy with the social environment, a nonconformity which leads him to renounce the world of men and to withdraw into his own private world to devote himself to his artistic pursuits.

Symbolism, to which Eguren made a late but valuable contribution, has been defined as "the art of expressing ideas and emotions not by describing them directly, nor by defining them through overt comparisons with concrete images, but by suggesting what those ideas and emotions are, by re-creating them in the mind of the reader through the use of unexplained symbols."[4] Symbolist writing, in other words, makes use of concrete objects not to represent ideas or emotions but rather to evoke them for the reader. The symbol is a comparison between the abstract and the concrete with one of the terms of the comparison being merely hinted at, and because the symbol thus frequently stands alone, with the reader being given little or no indication of what is being symbolised, Symbolist poetry inevitably has a certain built-in obscurity. Indeed, obscurity is deliberately sought after in the Symbolist aesthetic. The Symbolists regarded mystery as an essential quality of art, for they felt that the aesthetic pleasure of poetry derived largely from divining the poem's hidden depths little by little. Thus, Mallarmé contended that "to name an object is to banish the major part of the enjoyment derived from a poem, since this enjoyment consists in a process of gradual revelation."[5]

4. C. Chadwick, *Symbolism* (London: Methuen, 1971), pp.2-3. This paragraph paraphrases Chadwick.   5. Quoted by Chadwick, p.2.

Eguren's version of the Symbolist aesthetic is delineated in the poem already quoted. Its basis is formed by a myriad host of strange characters — the figures hunted by Peregrín — and his most distinctive poems are built around them.[6] The characters are frequently placed in remote settings — exotic lands such as the Orient or the Nordic countries, or an indeterminate past that is vaguely medieval — which detach them from reality as the reader knows it. The poems often take the form of anecdotes or dramatic vignettes. One of their outstanding features is their dynamism: the characters appear before us, pass in front of our eyes, and then disappear from view.[7] The best of them are characterised by their concision and objectivity: the poet limits himself to presenting the characters to us and rarely intervenes to comment or to give us clues as to how we should interpret the poems. The poems, in other words, operate firstly on an immediate level as versified tales or character sketches with no apparent reference to anything but themselves. At the same time, however, the characters embody in synthesised form "las emociones más intensas de mi vida" which Eguren sought to "exteriorizar" in his verse[8] and, by the manner of their presentation, they point to another reality hidden beneath the surface of the poem. His poetry, therefore, often appears to be simple and straightforward, but is, in fact, extremely difficult to penetrate.

Eguren's Symbolism, like that of Mallarmé, rests to a large extent on the conviction that mystery is an indispensable ingredient for aesthetic pleasure. The dynamism of his poetry, for example, corresponds to a belief that static beauty soon loses its enchantment since it can be grasped and known in its entirety.[9] It is probable, however, that there is another facet to his Symbolism. In a revealing portrait Enrique Carrillo describes Eguren as a man who always concealed his feelings behind the mask of a gentle, melancholy smile:

> Es un fiero y noble artista, que vive encerrado en su propio ideal como en una *turris eburnea*; en quien desengaños, amarguras, afanes, ansias de perfectabilidad, choques con el torpe mundo exterior e incertidumbres y desfallecimientos íntimos se disimulan siempre tras una sonrisa suave y algo triste . . .[10]

---

6. César A. Debarbieri, in his *Los personajes en la poética de José María Eguren* (Lima: Departamento de Humanidades, Universidad del Pacífico, 1975), examines no less than sixty-six different characters in Eguren's poetry and even then his study is incomplete.   7. See Debarbieri, p.28.
8. Eguren, p.421.   9. "La estética se funda en el movimiento . . . He visto pasar velozmente bellezas inexpresables, que una vez quietas y fijas han perdido su encantadora celestía . . . lo estático es una especie de muerte" (236-7).
10. E.A. Carrillo, "Ensayo sobre José María Eguren", in J.M. Eguren, *La canción de las figuras* (Lima: Tipografía y Encuadernación de la Penitenciaría, 1916), p.8.

In the same way, it seems to me, his Symbolism serves to mask his feelings as well as to express them. Eguren is not a poet who lays bare his soul to the public gaze, but rather one who hides his inner self from the eyes of a world he distrusts and reveals himself only to those who are sensitive enough to understand him.

Eguren was a quiet, gentle, timid man, obviously ill-equipped for the social life, and he has tended to be regarded as a naïve and unworldly aesthete who was blissfully unaware of what was going on around him. Several of his poems, however, seem to be commentaries on the contemporary world. They suggest that he viewed the society of his day with a critical eye and that his withdrawal into seclusion was the result not only of a temperamental inadaptability but of a conscious rejection of the values of that society. Though not one of his better poems, "Colonial" (107) is interesting as an example of his social awareness. It is also an example of how even his simplest poems have deceived the critics. Debarbieri regards the female protagonist as "la exponente por antonomasia del espíritu criollo de la mujer limeña" and for him the poem recreates the traditional picture of the *limeña* as beautiful, graceful, gay, playful and coquettish.[11] In fact, if *la rubia ambarina* is the embodiment of Limeñan womanhood, she incarnates the worst features of the species, and the effect of the poem's viceregal setting is to suggest that the tradition is a myth that has come down from colonial times and which was never true. The protagonist is indeed gay and playful, but her playfulness expresses itself in cruel acts that verge on sadism. Her idea of a practical joke is to feign suicide so that she might enjoy the spectacle of her family's distress. Even her coquetry is perverse, for she employs her charms to seduce the vicereine's lover, merely for the pleasure of stealing another woman's man and outdoing an exalted rival. When her advances are disregarded, she withdraws in a fit of pique and after nursing her spite in alcoholic brooding, vents it by setting fire to the drapings. *La rubia ambarina* appears, in short, as spoilt, selfish, cruel and vindictive, and she reveals a less flattering side to the traditional image of Limeñan womanhood. Eguren here anticipates Sebastián Salazar Bondy's assault, in *Lima la horrible*, on the complacent myths *limeños* hold about the nature of their society.[12] The poem is clear proof that he understood only too well the kind of world he was opting out of.

11. Debarbieri, p.46.
12. Sebastián Salazar Bondy, *Lima la horrible* (México: Era, 1964).

In opting out, however, Eguren was not merely turning his back on Limeñan society but repudiating the values on which Western civilisation is based. No less than his European contemporaries he saw and was appalled by the evils caused by Western man's aggressive urge to conquer and dominate. In "El caballo" (54) a horse comes back from the dead only to discover to its horror that, in the centuries that have elapsed since it met its death on the battlefield, humanity has learned nothing from its mistakes and is still engaged in bloody strife:

> Viene por las calles,
> a la luna parva,
> un caballo muerto
> en antigua batalla.
>
> Sus cascos sombríos . . .
> trepida, resbala;
> da un hosco relincho,
> con sus voces lejanas.
>
> En la plúmbea esquina
> de la barricada,
> con ojos vacíos
> y con horror, se para.
>
> Más tarde se escuchan
> sus lentas pisadas,
> por vías desiertas,
> y por ruinosas plazas.

The poem goes further and implies that insofar as there has been change it has been for the worse. The representative of an age of chivalry when knights fought in single combat, the horse finds itself completely out of place in an urban environment where it is confronted by barricades that belong to an age of mass warfare in which the individual is merely cannon fodder and entire cities are laid waste. Humanity, the poem suggests, has progressed only in the sense that it has learned to kill more efficiently and to wreak greater devastation.

Eguren seems to have foreseen that in our times the aggressiveness inherent in the Western way of life would lead to a new Dark Age in which barbaric forces of oppression would turn on the very civilisation which had spawned them. He saw, too, that in its complacency humanity was blind to the danger. "El andarín de la noche" (131) introduces a mysterious figure who journeys the length and breadth of the land warning people of the approach of war. No one heeds him and the country is invaded, devastated and enslaved:

> En la batalla cayó la torre;
> siguieron ruinas, desolaciones;
> canes sombríos
> buscan los muertos en los caminos.

> Suenan los bombos y las trompetas
> y las picotas y las cadenas;
> y nadie ha visto, por el confín;
> nadie recuerda
> al andarín.

The climax reveals that the citizens were so oblivious to danger that not only was the warning ignored but no one even recalls seeing the herald of doom. Published in 1929, the poem is an eloquent commentary on the events of the following decade.

Anticipating Miguel Angel Asturias' *El Señor Presidente*, the poem "La ronda de espadas" (94) reads like a premonition of the barbaric totalitarianism that was to degrade Europe and America in the course of the twentieth century. Though set in medieval times, it is in fact a vision of the oppressive atmosphere of a modern police state. It introduces a typical medieval institution, the town guard, whose job it was to patrol the streets at night, preserve the peace and protect the citizenry, but, as Debarbieri has observed,[13] the role of guard in the poem is the reverse of what it ought to be. Instead of inspiring a sense of security, the echo of their footsteps and the jingle of their weapons spread fear and panic. In the poem, therefore, the forces of law and order have become forces of oppression. It is noteworthy that the guard is referred to throughout as "la ronda de espadas": they are seen not as individuals nor even as men, but as a sinister, inhuman and impersonal armed force.

The opening stanza establishes an atmosphere of menace and terror. In the darkness the armour and swords of the guard glint sinisterly in the moonlight, and the roads leading in and out of the city have been cut off by fear, so that it is as if terror had the city under siege:

> Por las avenidas,
> de miedo cercadas,
> brilla en noche de azules oscuros,
> la ronda de espadas.

In the following stanzas a growing tension is built up as the poem keeps cutting back and forth between the marching guard and the frightened citizenry:

> Duermen los postigos,
> las viejas aldabas;
> y se escuchan borrosas de canes
> las músicas bravas.

---

13. Debarbieri, p.82.

Ya los extramuros
y las arruinadas
callejuelas, vibrante ha pasado
la ronda de espadas.

Y en los cafetines
que el humo amortaja,
al sentirla el tahur de la noche,
cierra la baraja.

Por las avenidas
morunas, talladas,
viene lenta, sonora, creciente
la ronda de espadas.

The townsfolk are behind closed doors and the barking of the dogs is muted. Even the hardened gamblers of the taverns put away their cards at the sound of the guard's approach. The whole town is in the grip of fear and seems to be holding its breath as it waits and listens apprehensively. There is an ominous dynamism in the poem as it traces the progress of the guard through the city, from the outskirts through the old quarter to the elegant city centre. The insistent repetition of the title phrase at the end of every alternate stanza creates an impression of inexorable marching, and the tension becomes almost unbearable in the fifth stanza where a climactic enumeration of adjectives suggests the echo of slow but relentless footsteps which grow louder and louder as the guard draws nearer and nearer.

In this oppressive atmosphere it is with relief that we reach the sixth stanza which introduces a refuge of beauty and tenderness in a world of menace and fear:

Tras las celosías,
esperan las damas
paladines que traigan de amores
las puntas de llamas.

Behind the shutters of their boudoirs the ladies are dreaming of the lovers who will come to win their hearts and claim their love. But no sooner has this oasis of love been evoked than it is put in jeopardy. The following stanza brings the tension of the poem to its climax as, with a great clatter of arms and stamping of feet, the guard comes to a sudden halt beneath the ladies' balconies:

Bajo los balcones
do están encantadas,
se detiene, con súbito ruido,
la ronda de espadas.

The narration ends at this point and there is an ominous silence before Eguren brings the poem to a conclusion. Rather than describe what has happened, the final stanzas express the horror of the poet at events too terrible to be narrated. Instead of meeting their lovers the ladies have met their deaths at the hands of the guard:

> Tristísima noche
> de nubes extrañas:
> ¡ay, de acero las hojas lucientes
> se tornan guadañas!
> ¡Tristísima noche
> de las encantadas!

What makes the conclusion of this poem so terrifying is that no explanation is given for the slaying of the ladies. All we know is that their longing to love and be loved has been answered by brutality and that beauty and tenderness have been stamped out. We are in a world ruled by intimidation and terror and where human values are trodden underfoot.

Eguren evidently felt that our civilisation had taken a wrong direction and one which would ultimately lead to its destruction if it did not change course. His poetry abounds in gentle feminine figures who are the antithesis of the aggressive males of the poems just examined, and it would seem that he saw in the feminine values of love and tenderness an antidote to the evils of a male-dominated world. One such figure is the school-mistress of the poem "Tiza Blanca" (187). The opening stanzas establish her character by presenting her in terms of whiteness — seen in her dress, her cheeks, the "serene light" irradiating from her face — which is not only a reflection of her inner being but identifies her with the morning light warming and illuminating the world:

> A la prima luz del día
> candorosa se vestía
> de piqué bordado fino,
> cinturón alabastrino.
> Iba a clase, a las lecciones
> con sus ojos pupilones,
> con su clara luz serena,
> sus mejillas de azucena.

The kindness she brings to her teaching takes material form in the sweets and pastries she carries to school for the children, and it wins their trust and affection and creates an atmosphere of warmth and harmony. Fighting, punishments and boredom have all been banished from her classroom, and her gentle, kindly approach clarifies the mysteries of learning in such a way that even the dullest pupils flourish in understanding:

> Si al tablero se acercaba
> con la tiza conversaba.
> A su vera los negados
> florecían avisados.
> Los libraba de enemigos,
> horas lentas y castigos.
> Era el campo, la blancura,
> del colegio la Ternura.

The affectionate nickname by which she is known to her pupils sums up all that she is and means to them, for the chalk is not merely the image of her limpid character but is the instrument by which she projects her inner self and guides them towards understanding. As a symbol of the character and the values she embodies, the chalk stands in stark contrast to the swords wielded by the guard to coerce the citizens in "La ronda de espadas". If, in that poem, the town held in the grip of terror is the image of what lies in store for a world where men blindly continue to pursue their urge to dominate one another, the classroom is here the image of what the world ought to be and what it might be if they learned to approach one another with love and understanding.

Eguren also believed that Western civilisation had stifled man's natural vitality and he saw in its inhibiting bourgeois values a denial of life itself. In "Las bodas vienesas" (18) such values are ridiculed in the persons of stern, puritanical aunts and withered old maids, whose fear of letting their hair down is amusingly underlined by their occasional lapses into tipsiness:

> preséntanse mustias las primas beodas . . .
> y rígidas, fuertes, las tías Amelias.

"Blasón" (21) is a delicious satire of bourgeois morality. Written in the style of a children's tale, it narrates the downfall of a young innocent princess who dreams romantic dreams of love in her castle tower, only to be seduced by a predatory lecherer who, at the approach of the royal household, abandons her and makes good his escape. The girl's governesses, seeing their oft repeated warnings unheeded and their worst fears realised, wring their hands and bewail her undoing:

> A niña que dulces amores sueña
> la persigue el Duque de los halcones;
> y si no mienten las fablas de dueña,
> se acercan doradas tribulaciones . . .
>
> Vienen la coja reina y los nobles;
> raudo el Duque procura alejamiento;
> pero las ayas de los fustes dobles,
> la aurora predicen del sufrimiento.

The effectiveness of the poem proceeds from the fact that it ironically adopts the governesses' viewpoint in order to deride it. Sheltered and protected, the girl had hitherto inhabited an artificial ideal world of dreams and, though she has come to know pain and sorrow and though she may regret the loss of her virginity and her innocence, her seduction, nonetheless, marks her first experience of love and life. She has come alive for the first time, for to live is to experience life's duality, to suffer its pains as well as to savour its joys. To cosset oneself against pain is to stifle life itself, and the fears, precautions and lamentations of the queen and her household are symptomatic of the bourgeois' negative approach to living. It is significant that the queen should be lame, for her physical deformity is the outward sign of her distorted values and of the stunted life which results from them.

Like "Blasón", many of Eguren's poems have the form of children's fantasy tales. Set in an indeterminate past, they are peopled by stock figures — kings, queens, nobles — who appear as grotesque marionettes caught in stereotyped postures and performing ritual gestures. Courtiers strut by like peacocks:

> Vienen túmidos y erguidos palaciegos borgoñones
> (12)

Great lords bow to one another with exaggerated ceremony:

> los magnates postradores,
> aduladores,
> al suelo el penacho inclinan. (36)

Senile old men ("cretinos ancianos") (18), and sexless, moustachioed old women ("ambiguas, / añosas marquesas") (30), hobble past as moribund examples of a society that has been drained of all vitality. It is likely that Eguren deliberately used the medium of the children's fantasy tale to mirror the adult world and that the grotesquely conventional nobility of these poems is intended in part to parody contemporary society, which he saw as being equally decadent. He seems to have regarded the modern age as one in which life had been fossilised by convention, an age in which men had lost the capacity to live life with illusion and enthusiasm. In "El dominó" (37) this spiritual bankruptcy is personified by yet another aristocratic character from the past. The setting is the gay, noisy atmosphere of the Mardi Gras festivities: it is a night of "unfathomable marvels" and in the streets the common people are laughing, dancing and singing. Against this background the protagonist is introduced in his lonely room. In a grotesque attempt to participate in the general festivity he has dressed up in a masquerade costume and has had the table set for a feast at which he plays the host to imaginary guests whom he invites by signs to be seated and to take up their glasses:

> Alumbraron en la mesa los candiles,
> moviéronse solos los aguamaniles,
> y un dominó vacío, pero animado,
> mientras ríe por la calle la verbena,
> se sienta, iluminado,
> y principia la cena.

> Su clara antifaz de un amarillo frío
> da los espantos en derredor sombrío
> esta noche de insondables maravillas,
> y tiende vagas, lucífugas señales
> a los vasos, las sillas
> de ausentes comensales.

He is not able to keep up this pathetic pretence for long, however, and at the end of the poem he abandons the table in despair, horrified and conscience-stricken at his inability to share in the joys and pleasures of ordinary folk, to commune with his fellows in the feast of life:

> Y luego en horror que nacarado flota,
> por la alta noche de voluptad ignota,
> en la luz olvida manjares dorados,
> ronronea una oración culpable, llena
> de acentos desolados,
> y abandona la cena.

It will be noted that Eguren does not present his character as a person of flesh and blood but as an empty costume: like Eliot's hollow men, he is the mere appearance of a human being with no real existence. In the light of the candle his mask glows with the chill yellowness of death and he casts off rays which are like the emanation of a spectre. He is in fact a man spiritually dead, a man whose existence is such an absurd parody of living that he himself realises the futility of continuing to go through the motions. The domino, in short, is the image of a social order that has been sapped of its vitality and has lost the simple ability to live.

It is significant that much of Eguren's poetry should be concerned with children and with the creatures of the wild — animals, birds, insects —, for, uninhibited by the pressures of civilisation, they epitomise the natural zest for living which bourgeois society has lost. Thus, "Efímera" (78) is a song to the mayfly which lives to the full every moment of its brief twenty-four hour existence. As it darts about gaily over the waters of the lake, its flight is like an exuberant dance expressing the joy of being alive:

> Por las aguas doradas dichosa vuelas
> celebrando la vida, con tarantelas.

It flits from water-lily to water-lily, flirting with each of them and then moving on, deaf to the recriminations of the flowers who reproach it for its fickleness:

> Y desoyes la culpa de las ninfeas
> por los juegos de amores que centelleas.

The mayfly, in fact, is never static but dashes through life in a "fuga loca", frantically grasping after fresh experience as if fearful of wasting a precious second. Such is its zeal to experience everything that it stretches its wings and flies eagerly into the gathering darkness that signifies its death:

> En tus celos las alas tiendes veloces
> a la naciente imagen que desconoces.

Far from fearing death, it is attracted to it as a new unknown area of experience to be explored. The mayfly is, therefore, a lesson to man that life is not to be feared but a fragile and precious gift to be enjoyed to the utmost.

Eguren, then, seems to have regarded our civilisation as bankrupt in that modern man had lost his natural vitality while retaining his primitive aggressiveness. Yet there is another aspect of modern life which disturbed him even more and which takes us to the heart of his work. In common with Carlyle, Ruskin and the German Idealists, he felt that the sickness of our civilisation had its roots above all in modern man's want of a religious sense, in his blindness to the sacred nature of the world and to life's essential spirituality. A key poem in this context is "El dios cansado" (58). The poem introduces an exhausted deity who can no longer cope and it takes us with him on a tour of barren deserts, atheistic regions and cities given over to darkness, through a world that regards him with indifference and is even unaware of his existence:

> Plomizo, carminado
> y con la barba verde,
> el ritmo pierde
> el dios cansado.
>
> Y va con tristes ojos,
> por los desiertos rojos,
> de los beduinos
> y peregrinos.
>
> Sigue por las obscuras
> y ciegas capitales
> de negros males
> y desventuras.

Reinante el día estuoso,
camina sin reposo
tras los inventos
y pensamientos.

Continúa, ignorado
por la región atea;
y nada crea
el dios cansado.

The weary god may be interpreted firstly as a symbol of the old god in whom men can no longer believe, of the old religion which has worn itself out and become fossilised in ritual and dogma. Yet the poem also hints that God has changed his nature, that, in an attempt to win men back to faith in him, he has made himself a god of progress, scouring the world for ideas and inventions which would restore him to favour in men's eyes. But not only does he fail to win men's allegiance, but by his inability to create he demonstrates that he has been dispossessed of his divinity. The impotent god, therefore, is also a symbol of the new faith that has replaced the old religion, the positivistic cult of scientific and material progress which denies the power of God and the very existence of spiritual forces in the universe. Needless to say, the weary god is also the image of modern man who, having lost faith in traditional religious creeds, has cast around him for a new centre for his existence and has turned to science. In so doing he has gone astray, for, since the new faith takes no account of spiritual realities, he has lost his "rhythm", his sense of spiritual harmony with his world. The poem implies that if man is to find his way again, he must regain the religious sense of earlier ages, without necessarily turning back to the old gods. To the mechanistic world-view of our times Eguren opposes a spiritual view of the cosmos.

The air of mystery with which Eguren seeks to imbue his poetry corresponds not only to his aesthetic but also to a conviction that "la condición humana es el misterio" (243), that the universe we live in is a great mystery which our reason can never penetrate. Thus, in "Alas" (116) the enigma of life is embodied in the migrant birds who emerge out of the skies from some remote land on their way to some equally unknown destination. In the markings on their plumage the poet sees an esoteric language holding the key to the secret of existence but it is a language which men are unable to decipher:

Tienen en sus pennas extrañas figuras
cual de las ignotas artes y escrituras.

The misty or nocturnal settings which are a feature of so many poems help to build up a sense of a mysterious, incomprehensible universe.

In "Nocturno" (55) the night shrouding the world in darkness becomes a symbol of the mystery that envelops all things:

> Y las cosas, los hombres domina
> la parda señora,
> de brumosos cabellos flotantes
> y negra corona.

In "Véspera" (174) it is the realm of the unknown forces which govern life:

> La bruma empantalla
> los faroles del mar,
> sueñan las brisas
> y en el silencio
> aletean
> las obscuras Causas.

Eguren clearly dismisses the pretensions of a scientific age to explain and understand the cosmos by reducing it to mechanistic principles, and he would have concurred with Carlyle's assertion that "it is a poor science that would hide from us the great deep sacred infinitude of Nescience, whither we can never penetrate, on which all science swims as a mere superficial film."[14]

In the passage just quoted Carlyle goes on to add: "This world, after all our science and sciences, is still a miracle; wonderful, inscrutable, *magical* and more, to whosoever will *think* of it." In the same spirit Eguren responds with wonder, awe and reverence to the mystery surrounding him, for life he regards as something miraculous and the world as a magical place. Their sensibilities dulled by habit, most men take the objects around them for granted, but Eguren's poetry expresses "el asombro ante la existencia de las cosas."[15] Poems like "Marginal" (57), "Las niñas de luz" (81) and "Princesita" (199) register his delight in the marvels of nature as if he were seeing them for the first time. In "Vespertina" (165) the spectacle of a butterfly provokes a panegyric of admiration:

> Crepuscular mariposa
> galana, maravillosa,
> topacio de las aldeas,
> la diva de los pinares
> y las alteas.

Moreover, for Eguren such marvels attest to a spiritual presence behind the veil of appearances and in his poetry the material universe is animated by spiritual forces. The abandoned house of "Casa vetusta" (15)

---

14. Thomas Carlyle, *On Heroes and Hero Worship* (London: Everyman, 1967), pp.245-6.
15. Julio Ortega, *Figuración de la persona* (Barcelona: EDHASA, 1970), p.102.

is peopled by spirits, and the migrant storks who make their annual stop there swap reminiscences about its former inhabitants:

> En su raro aposento
> viven las hadas
> y los antiguos seres
> de la campaña.
> Las ancianas cigüeñas
> que en ella paran
> de los muertos señores
> a veces hablan.

In "Los robles" (35) the idyllic peace of the countryside draws childlike tears of pleasure from the trees:

> En la curva del camino
> dos robles lloraban como dos niños.
> Y había paz en los campos,
> y en la mágica luz del cielo santo.

Trees, birds and insects join in a pantheistic prayer in "La oración del monte" (59):

> Reza el olmo secular,
> el afligido sinsonte
> y el insecto militar.

Thus, in defiance of the positivistic thought of his time Eguren considers visible objects to be but the manifestation of a greater spiritual reality.

Psychic phenomena held a peculiar fascination for Eguren and he himself underwent a number of experiences which seemed to him to confound the natural laws. "Noche I" (79) describes one such experience which occurred on the occasion of the death of a niece. The girl, who had been ill with tuberculosis, had been moved to Jauja on the "puna helada" in the hope that the purer air would aid recovery, but in fact she died there. One night the poet, sick with anxiety, was pacing restlessly up and down in his room when he sensed footsteps near him which he recognised as those of his niece, and this, he realised, was the girl's spirit attempting to communicate with him as it departed from this world:

> Y en tu pálida agonía,
> me dijiste que vendría . . .
> tu alma a ver mi desventura . . .
> y en la noche quemadora de la mente,
> sólo llegan, tristemente,
> ¡ay, tus pasos!, ¡ay, tus pasos!

As it turned out, the girl's death did in fact coincide with this experience in seeming confirmation of the existence of psychic forces.[16]

---

16. Debarbieri, p.86, claims that the poem was written on the very night the girl died. It is more likely that the poem is merely a dramatisation of the experience.

Elsewhere he speaks of occasions on which he communed with the dead. In "Noche II" (99) he summons up a spirit from the other world who identifies herself to him as Danira and tells him the story of her life, but when he questions her about life beyond the grave and asks for news of his dead beloved she retreats into the shadows. The essay "Noche azul" (320) recounts how the spirit of his dead beloved appeared to him in the night: "Una haz de niebla se asomó por el acantilado y transpuso la baranda. Era mi amada, del pasado; un arrayán de sueño, un vaporoso anuncio de otros días ... Estás junto a mí en las sombras, pero es matutino tu perfume. Eres un clavel que Dios me ha dado para consolarme de las miradas grises." Similarly, in "Visiones de enero" (147), returning to the old *hacienda* where he used to spend vacations, he encounters a nebulous apparition from the spirit world which he recognises as a young girl from his childhood whose life was tragically cut short.

Eguren was also fascinated by the phenomenon of dreaming in which the human spirit, liberated from the limitations of the everyday world and the constraints of reason, wanders freely through a marvellous universe inaccessible to the conscious mind. This phenomenon is the theme of "Fantasía" (124) and "Los sueños" (130)' In the latter poem the darkened room is a symbol of the subconscious mind of the sleeping children into whose dream world we are introduced:

De noche, en la sala ceñida de brumas,
los sueños están;
en el viejo piano, con manos de plumas
festivas canciones a los niños dan.
Son mágicos sueños de mirar lontano
que, en azul tiniebla, tocan en el piano
la trova del viejo remoto andarín;
alegres, terminan la canción chinesca,
y luego preludían la jota grotesca,
gala del festín
del mandón Mandín.
Y el baile encantado,
el baile festivo azul, colorado
y de rosicler;
y luego la boda triunfal, la ventura
del príncipe de oro y la niña obscura
tocan con placer.
Los músicos sueños, antes de la aurora,
tocan en el piano fiesta encantadora,
los finos arpegios, rara melodía
que tiene el castillo de juguetería.
Mas cuando despunta el fulgor temprano

> y la sala llena de coloraciones,
> los sueños nocturnos se van piano, piano
> por la chimenea, ventanas, balcones.

Dreams are personified as magical, elf-like creatures who appear in the night and whose "distant gaze" goes beyond horizons and frontiers to conjure up for the children visions of remote and wonderful lands. They are also presented as musicians — for Eguren as for the French Symbolists music was supreme among the arts for its powers of evocation — whose melodies summon up, by a kind of magic that defies the laws of time and space, scenes from an assortment of countries and periods — the wanderings of the Medieval troubadours, the Orient, the kingdom of Aragón — and even from the imaginary world of fairy tales — the court of the mighty lord "mandón Mandín", the marriage of the humble girl to the handsome prince. But as day breaks the dreams scamper off, for night is their domain and light drives them away. In the waking world reason reasserts its tyranny over the mind, banishing such magical visions and confining our gaze to the limits of what can be seen and touched.

For Eguren psychic experiences and dreams indicate that there is a plane of reality beyond the material world which can only be apprehended by our irrational faculties. Thus, he states: "Esto prueba que nuestro entendimiento y nuestra razón son facultades limitadas a nuestro medio y que hay otro plano inaccesible donde nuestra razón cae en pedazos al tratar de abordar estos motivos, y de ello inferimos que nuestro entendimiento navega inrumbe, en nuestro plano tempestuoso" (319-20). It is perhaps significant that "Ananké" (17), "Flor de amor" (62) and "Las naves de la noche" (63) should refer to the loss of innocence and the unhappiness that accompanies it, for, though these poems treat the theme in a sexual context, they point to an assumption that underlies all of Eguren's work — the belief that modern man's sickness derives from the loss of his primitive innocence. Man has progressed in the sense that in developing his reasoning powers he has overcome his primitive awe and fear of the world and has dominated it through science and technology. Indeed, he has grown so confident of his own powers that he no longer recognises any power greater than himself, but, though he is too arrogant to see it, his progress has been one-dimensional and he has become atrophied in the process. For he has developed his reason at the cost of stunting his other faculties and in dominating the world he has lost all sense of its magic and wonder, all awareness of the spiritual reality behind the material. To become whole, Eguren believes, man must recover something of his lost innocence, he must rehabilitate his long neglected irrational faculties.

It is in this context that we should see a group of poems which take us into the world of Nordic mythology, poems such as "Eroe" (20), which recounts the burial of a character from the *Eddas* and her ascent into Valhalla, and "La Walkyria" (22), which presents one of the Valkyrs, the Choosers of the Slain, as the symbol of an inexorable destiny. For, more than exoticism, it was primitive man's response to his world that attracted the poet to such themes. Living in awe of a world ruled by forces he could not comprehend or tame, the ancient Norseman saw behind the workings of nature mysterious, invisible powers which he personified as gods and demons. Two poems take us inside the uncivilised mind. "El dios de la centella" (96) dramatises the panic and terror of the primitive at a shooting star which he interprets as a presage of the wrath of the god of thunder and lightning.[17] "Los gigantones" (162) evokes a fearful storm which breaks out over the mountains in the night. Thunder rumbles menacingly and lightning rends the skies, blasting trees with its bolts and setting them alight. The poem, however, does not describe the storm in these terms but as seen through terrified primitive eyes:

> En noche triste
> los gigantones de la montaña
> han encendido rojas fogatas.
>
> Hoy celebrando
> la Cordillera,
> con los semblantes iluminados,
> están de fiesta.
>
> Los gigantones de la montaña
> han encendido
> sus llamaradas.
>
> En triste noche
> cuando remotas suenan las quedas,
> bailan con roncos sonidos lentos
> y con la música de las peñas.
>
> Los gigantones
> cantan antiguas rondas salvajes
> y en las alturas
> las bacanales.
>
> Prenden los pinos y cocobolos
> ¡ay, de las niñas si están beodos!

17. The atmosphere of this poem, like that of the others mentioned, is Nordic except for the reference to the Chaldeans (1.9), a display of erudition that is inappropriate in the mouth of a primitive.

En roja noche
de vino agreste
¡ay, de la blonda
niña celeste!
Los gigantones de la montaña
han encendido
su llamarada.

Writing of Nordic mythology, Carlyle says: "The dark hostile powers of Nature they figure to themselves as 'Jötuns', Giants, huge shaggy beings of a demonic character. Frost, Fire, Sea-tempest; these are Jötuns."[18] Accordingly, in the poem, demon giants cavort and carouse around bonfires in a fiendish orgy before going on a drunken rampage in which they not only cause extensive material damage but threaten the virtue of the local maidens, a detail which highlights the extent to which the primitive mind saw the forces of nature as personal agencies. However, it is not so much the superstitions themselves as what lies behind them that is important in these poems. Eguren believed, like Carlyle, that the essence of Nordic mythology was "recognition of the Divineness of Nature; sincere communion of man with the mysterious invisible Powers visibly seen at work in the world around him."[19] Behind the obsolete beliefs of the ancients there is an awareness of a greater reality, and the superstitions are but the imperfect gropings of untutored men to explain that reality. For all his ignorance primitive man was aware of a truth to which modern man is blind in spite of all his science. The religious spirit behind the ancient superstitions, Eguren suggests, is just as valid today as it was in the remote past.

It is in a similar light that we are to understand Eguren's so-called "poemas infantiles". Apparently such poems were originally written for the amusement of the poet's own nephews and nieces and are, therefore, aimed at a child audience. On this level the best of them are remarkable *tours de force*. "El Duque" (36) is a fantasy tale which parts from a concrete reality. A group of children are seated around a table at a party, and to amuse them the poet weaves a story around the foodstuffs on the table: a walnut becomes the grandiose "duque Nuez" whose wedding serves as a pretext for parading before the children a procession of fabulous characters. The poem opens with a sing-song rhythm designed to involve the children in the story:

Hoy se casa el duque Nuez;
viene el chantre, viene el juez.

---

18. Carlyle, p.254.   19. Ibid., pp.226-7.

Thereafter everything in the poem is calculated to maintain their involvement. The magnificence of the "florid cavalcade" is emphasised to arouse their wonder and admiration. Haughty and mysterious knights — "Galo cetrino, Rodolfo montante" — ride past with "ceño triunfante", inspiring awe, while the sinister "Lobo del Monte", whose horses are covered with "pieles de bisonte", strikes a note of fear. Other characters provoke hilarity:

> los corvados, los bisiestos
> dan sus gestos, sus gestos, sus gestos;
> y la turba melenuda
> estornuda, estornuda, estornuda.

Then, when all the guests have been introduced, it is discovered that the only person not present is the Duke himself. The bride looks anxiously for his arrival and great lords go red in the face with indignation at being kept waiting:

> Y a los pórticos y a los espacios
> mira la novia con ardor; . . .
> son sus ojos dos topacios
> de brillor.
> Y hacen fieros ademanes,
> nobles rojos como alacranes;
> concentrando sus resuellos
> grita el más hercúleo de ellos:
> ¿Quién al gran Duque entretiene? . . .;
> ya el gran cortejo se irrita! . . .

Then, when suspense has been built up by this passage, when the children are holding their breath and wondering what is going to happen next, the poem resolves itself in laughter:

> Pero el Duque no viene; . . .
> se lo ha comido Paquita.

The story, it is revealed, was only a fantasy, the characters were merely foodstuffs, and the Duke cannot come to his wedding because one of the little girls has eaten him up.

"Juan Volatín" (39) is a dramatic, nail-biting tale about a bogyman. The opening stanzas build up an atmosphere of mystery and foreboding. A group of children are playing in a house while outside everything is dark and desolate and sinister. Suddenly the children sense danger and the bogyman bursts in on them through a window. As his name indicates, Juan Volatín is characterised by his speed and agility of movement which enable him to corner his victims no matter how they try to flee. Confronting the children, he boasts of his exploits as a purveyor of mischief and death and so terrifies them that they take to their heels and hide:

> ¡Todos se han ido!
> ¡Solo me quedo!
> ¡Por Dios qué miedo
> les he traído!

Seeing his victims slip out of his clutches, he strikes a decisive and aggressive pose and goes in search of them in a sinister game of hide-and-seek. He catches a glimpse of their feet under the table and calls on them to come out, for his fantastic agility cuts off all possibility of escape:

> vengan Pichines;
> que en volatines
> de varios modos
> yo espero a todos.

It seems all up for the children, but at that moment they are saved by the arrival of a kindly sylph, who comes riding on a feather, guided by fireflies and followed by armed squadrons of golden insects. Her very appearance is enough to knock the fight out of Juan Volatín who sinks to the ground in fear and confusion:

> Juan Volatín se muestra amilanado,
> Juan Volatín esconde su espadín,
> Juan Volatín confuso, avergonzado,
> se sienta con un medio volatín.

The sylph ignores him, however, and goes to comfort the children, caressing them to sleep and transporting them to the marvellous world of dreams:

> Les muestra paisajes
> de mundos risueños
> allá en misteriosos
> nublados de sueños.

Meanwhile, her army turns on the bogyman and the child audience, whose apprehension has given way to relief at her timely intervention, is able to relax and laugh at the discomfiture and humiliation of Juan Volatín, whose rump is a favourite target for the insects' stings:

> Y luego la turba
> de insectos atroces
> a Juan Volatines
> saludan a voces;
> y pronto los vemos
> picar a destajo
> pescuezo, joraba
> y abajo, y abajo.

In the final lines Juan Volatín hands over his cape and his sword in acknowledgement of defeat and grovels ignominiously on the floor in stark contrast to the imperious and energetic manner with which he first appeared:

¡Juan Volatín entrega su capelo!
¡Juan Volatín entrega su espadín!
Juan Volatín rodando por el suelo
redobla volatín y volatín.

The poem thus ends, like all fairy tales worthy of the name, with evil routed and good triumphant.

It would be a travesty, however, to consider such poems as being only for children.[20] They are also poems about children. A large part of the adult's enjoyment of "El Duque" derives from picturing a child's reaction to the tale. The poem is a trip from reality through the realms of fantasy and back to reality again, a trip on which the child becomes completely involved in the fantasy and responds to it with rapt wonder and awe. It thus highlights the child's capacity for illusion, for living on a plane other than the rational and for feeling the magic and marvel of things, and the adult reader is made aware of how much he has lost in growing up. It is, in short, a poem which inspires nostalgia for the lost innocence of childhood. The same may be said of "Juan Volatín". The rout of the bogyman corresponds to more than the conventions of the fairy tale. The bogyman is the exteriorisation of the child's irrational fears and what puts him to flight is the child's compensating faculty of illusion. The adult may be able to rationalise such fears away, but his rationalism also banishes the good fairies who would transport him to realms of magic.

Another key poem is "La niña de la lámpara azul" (51) whose protagonist seems to be a kind of personal deity whom Eguren raises up in opposition to the weary and impotent god portrayed in "El dios cansado":

En el pasadizo nebuloso
cual mágico sueño de Estambul,
su perfil presenta destelloso
la niña de la lámpara azul.

Agil y risueña se insinúa,
y su llama seductora brilla,
tiembla en su cabello la garúa
de la playa de la maravilla.

Con voz infantil y melodiosa
en fresco aroma de abedul,
habla de una vida milagrosa
la niña de la lámpara azul.

20. It was observed earlier that they are sometimes a vehicle for parodying adult society. On other occasions, as will emerge later, they are used as a medium to allegorise the human condition.

Con cálidos ojos de dulzura
y besos de amor matutino,
me ofrece la bella criatura
un mágico y celeste camino.
De encantación en un derroche,
hiende leda, vaporoso tul;
y me guía a través de la noche
la niña de la lámpara azul.

A young girl poised on the brink of adolescence and characterised by her gaiety, her freshness, her ingenuous love of all things, she represents the capacity to approach life with child-like illusion, to feel the wonder and magic of being alive. As the poet wanders disorientated through the shadowy corridor of spiritual darkness, she manifests herself to him as a luminous presence bearing the guiding light of illusion, and her stature grows as the illusion she personifies communicates itself to the poet. At first she is an imprecise figure, a profile flashing intermittently, but in the second stanza she insinuates herself into his attentions and her lamp burns seductively. Gradually imposing her presence, she becomes a dynamic figure by the end of the poem where her spells tear away the cloudy veil obscuring the poet's vision and she guides him through the darkness towards her realm of magic. To see the world as a magical place, the poem suggests, is the privilege of those who, unatrophied by life-sapping reason, are able to approach life with the child-like illusion embodied by the girl with the blue lamp. Eguren might well have adopted as his motto the words of Christ: "Except ye be converted, and become as little children, ye shall not enter into the kingdom of Heaven" (Matthew 18.3). For underlying all his work is the conviction that man must recover the spiritual innocence of children and primitive peoples if he is to overcome his alienation and live once more in harmony with the world.

2

CESAR VALLEJO

Of all the Peruvian poets none has experienced alienation more keenly nor expressed it better than César Vallejo (1892-1938).[1] Two poems from *Trilce* take us to the heart of his work. In poem XLVII (189) memories of the trauma of birth rise from the poet's subconscious as he drowses. What is recalled are the rigidity of the foetus, which seems reluctant to abandon the security of the womb, and the eyes, which the newborn keeps tightly closed as if refusing to face the world:

> Duras todavía las articulaciones
> al camino, como cuando nos instan
> y nosotros no cedemos por nada . . .

> Los párpados cerrados, como si, cuando, nacemos
> siempre no fuese tiempo todavía.

The final lines associate the clumsy hands stretched out by the child with those of a drowning man groping for something to save him:

> Y las manitas que se abarquillan
> asiéndose de algo flotante,
> a no querer quedarse.

The same sense of helplessness is also expressed in poem III (145), a dramatic monologue based on an episode from the poet's infancy. The parents have gone out for the afternoon and, as night falls and there is still no sign of their return, the child Vallejo grows more and more uneasy. Frightened of venturing with the elder children out into the yard where ghosts prowl about in the shadows, and equally frightened of being left on his own, he sagely warns them to stay indoors and wait patiently for their parents to return:

> Aguedita, Nativa, Miguel,
> cuidado con ir por ahí, por donde
> acaban de pasar gangueando sus memorias
> dobladoras penas,

---

1. Vallejo is the author of four books of poetry: *Los heraldos negros* (1919), *Trilce* (1922), *Poemas humanos* and *España, aparta de mí este cáliz*. The last two were published posthumously as a single volume in 1939. All references are to the *Obra poética completa* (Lima: Moncloa, 1968).

> hacia el silencioso corral, y por donde
> las gallinas que se están acostando todavía,
> se han espantado tanto.
> Mejor estemos aquí no más.
> Madre dijo que no demoraría.

But while he is talking the others disappear and when he discovers that he is shut up alone in the dark house, he cries after them in panic:

> Aguedita, Nativa, Miguel?
> Llamo, busco al tanteo en la oscuridad.
> No me vayan a haber dejado solo,
> y el único recluso sea yo.

Either of these two poems might be regarded as an emblem of all Vallejo's poetry, for the poetic persona he most consistently adopts is that of a child stranded alone and defenceless in a dark, incomprehensible and menacing world.

Vallejo's alienation has to be understood partly in the context of his own personal experience. He grew up in a large, close-knit family in a small, isolated rural community in the heart of the Peruvian Andes. Leaving home to make good, he lived most of his adult life in large cities where he felt out of his element and, not surprisingly, his poetry is dominated by a sense of inadequacy and insecurity, by a feeling that he is a boy in a man's world, a world which is just too big for him to cope with. In Lima he was to suffer the homesickness of a lonely *serrano* immigrant, an experience which is recorded in several poems of *Trilce*. Poem XIV (156), as David Gallagher has observed,[2] summarises the reaction of the recently arrived provincial intimidated by the strange new world of the capital. Totally unprepared for the reality he encounters there, he is bewildered and overwhelmed. Even though he is aware that life in Lima has all the falsity of a circus and that the *limeños'* air of self-confident *machismo* is mere show, he cannot help but be intimidated by the frightening world in which he finds himself and through which they stroll with the strutting assurance of trapeze artists crossing a void. He is overawed by

> Esa manera de caminar por los trapecios.
> Esos corajosos brutos como postizos.

However, what appals him most about Lima is its falsity, typified by the commercialisation of love and by the contraceptives which deny love its full expression:

> Esta goma que pega el azogue al adentro.
> Esas posaderas sentadas para arriba.

---

2. D.P. Gallagher, *Modern Latin American Literature* (London-Oxford-New York: Oxford Univ. Press, 1973), p.24.

> Ese no puede ser, sido.
> Absurdo.
> Demencia.

To the bewildered provincial it seems that the whole natural order has been turned on its head in this city where the unthinkable is commonplace. His arrival in Lima, therefore, marks his initiation into a seemingly absurd and senseless world whose meaning escapes him. But at least, he concludes sarcastically, he has the satisfaction of having realised the ambitious provincial's dream of coming to Lima to make his fortune:

> Pero he venido de Trujillo a Lima.
> Pero gano un sueldo de cinco soles.

The final deflating irony makes it clear that in economic as well as emotional terms his venture to the capital has proved a fiasco.

Poem XLIX (191) expresses the loneliness and uneasiness felt by the poet as, sorrowfully wearing his newly acquired manhood like an ill-fitting suit trailing at the ankles, he confronts the moment of truth when he must fend for himself in the competitive commercial world:

> Murmurado en inquietud, cruzo,
> el traje largo de sentir, los lunes
>   de la verdad.
> Nadie me busca ni me reconoce,
> y hasta yo he olvidado
>   de quién seré.

In this strange, intimidating city where he knows no one, life becomes an empty routine of eating and working for no other purpose than to stay alive:

> Todos los días amanezco a ciegas
> a trabajar para vivir; y tomo el desayuno
> sin probar ni gota de él, todas las mañanas.   (198)

Back home in the *sierra* breakfast, served up by his mother and partaken with the family in a kind of communion of love, set the tone for the luminous days of his childhood, but here, eaten alone in a world unlit by love, it is merely the beginning of yet another day of a life that has lost its savour. Hence the lonely exile seeks to satisfy his thirst for love wherever and in whatever way he can, in the brothels or in casual sex:

> Regocíjate, huérfano; bebe tu copa de agua
> desde la pulpería de una esquina cualquiera.   (213)

A series of poems traces the ups-and-downs of a love affair which momentarily reproduced the domestic bliss the poet had known as a child, only to leave him in unhappy loneliness once again when the couple were separated by the girl's family:

> Hubo un día tan rico el año pasado . . . ! . . .
> Por esto nos separarán,
> por eso y para que ya no hagamos mal . . .
> por haber sido niños y también
> por habernos juntado mucho en la vida,
> reclusos para siempre nos irán a encerrar. (216)

Adopting once again the persona of a child to convey the incomprehensible coldness and cruelty of the world, the poet presents their affair as an innocent childish escapade which, unwittingly offending against some code of right and wrong which he does not understand, has inexplicably brought the wrath of the adults down on their heads, so that it seems to him that they have been separated and punished for no other reason than that they have committed the sin of being happy together. Thus in *Trilce* coastal Lima, arid and shrouded in grey mist, becomes the image of a loveless world, the very antithesis of the home in Santiago which his mother watched over lovingly, like the mountains watering the green, fertile valleys of the Northern *sierra*:

> Oh valle sin altura madre, donde todo duerme
> horrible mediatinta, sin ríos frescos, sin entradas
> de amor. (206)

Trilce, therefore, becomes a lament for the passing of the childhood which the poet left behind him in Santiago and which was brought to a definitive end by the death of his mother in 1918:

> Y se acabó el diminutivo, para
> mi mayoría en el dolor sin fin
> y nuestro haber nacido así sin causa. (176)

In a personal version of the myth of paradise lost his provincial home, seen from the perspective of distance, becomes an idyll to be evoked with nostalgia, a norm for measuring the world of the present and underlining its deficiencies. The axis of that happy, integrated world where his childhood unfolded in an atmosphere of peace, love and security, was the archetypal figure of the mother, the purveyor of life, love and nourishment. In poem XXIII (165) she is so associated in the poet's memory with the oven from which she brought forth a seemingly inexhaustible supply of biscuits that she becomes one with it. Radiating warmth, she nourished her family emotionally with her love at the same time as she gave sustenance to their bodies. Hence her biscuits are recalled by the poet as the stuff of life, the very essence of childhood:

> Tahona estuosa de aquellos mis bizcochos
> pura yema infantil innumerable, madre.

The distribution of the biscuits was a ceremony that had all the solemnity and significance of the Christian communion and in the timeless world of the myth life was regulated by that twice-daily ritual:

> En la sala de arriba nos repartías
> de manaña, de tarde, de dual estiba,
> aquellas ricas hostias de tiempo, para
> que ahora nos sobrasen
> cáscaras de relojes en flexión de las 24
> en punto parados.

But now, in the temporal present, clocks measure out the minutes and seconds that are but indigestible chaff left over from that eternal past, and in so doing, as if they were the empty shells of clocks that had come to a stop, they mark the end of true time.[3] Cast out of the childhood paradise, the poet must now struggle for survival in a competitive world where nothing is given freely out of love and everything must be fought and paid for:

> Tal la tierra oirá en tu silenciar,
> cómo nos van cobrando todos
> el alquiler del mundo donde nos dejas
> y el valor de aquel pan inacabable.

Still a child in the bewildering world of the adult, the poet is unable to understand why, having been given existence by his mother, he must now be made to pay for it, and with the aggrieved tone of one ill-done to, he appeals to her to vouch that he has not usurped his place in the world but is entitled to it by right of inheritance:

> Y nos lo cobran, cuando, siendo nosotros
> pequeños entonces, como tú verías,
> no se lo podíamos haber arrebatado
> a nadie; cuando tú nos los diste,
> ¿di, mamá?

Unfortunately, his dead mother is no longer in a position either to resolve his doubts or to right his wrongs. The persona of the child thus develops naturally into that of the orphan abandoned to his own resources.

Vallejo's belief in the world's arbitrary cruelty was confirmed by his three and half month's imprisonment and in "Trilce XVIII" (160) the prison cell becomes a symbol of the heartless world where he is now trapped. Seen in numerical terms, the walls of his cell stand as a symbol of the existential limitations imposed by a coldly rational world whose implacable laws deny him emotional fulfilment:

> Oh las cuatro paredes de la celda.
> Ah las cuatro paredes albicantes
> que sin remedio dan al mismo número.

3. The phrase "cáscaras de relojes" is a good example of the ambiguity which often enriches Vallejo's poetry. It simultaneously conjures up a vision of "husks of time" and "shells of clocks".

Since his mother is no longer there to succour him, the walls seem to him to take on the shape of dead mothers leading children down the slopes of the past, and thus come to symbolise the barriers cutting him off from the idyll of childhood and confining him in unhappy adulthood:

> De ellas me duelen entretanto más
> las dos largas que tienen esta noche
> algo de madres que ya muertas
> llevan por bromurados declives,
> a un niño de la mano cada una.

A helpless orphan, he remains emotionally attached to his dead mother while desperately needing someone to take her place. While one hand reaches back into the past, clinging to his mother, the other is raised aloft, groping for someone who will watch over him as she did:

> Ya sólo yo me voy quedando,
> con la diestra, que hace por ambas manos,
> en alto, en busca de terciario brazo
> que ha de pupilar, entre mi donde y mi cuando,
> esta mayoría inválida de hombre.

Adulthood is an invalid state since he now has to fend for himself in a world which makes him feel inadequate.

However, Vallejo's alienation must also be seen in relation to the general spiritual crisis of our times, in the context of modern man's loss of faith in the religious and philosophical assumptions which previously gave human existence a meaning within a universal order. His first volume, *Los heraldos negros*, expresses the metaphysical anguish of a young man who is no longer able to accept the religious beliefs in which he was brought up. In "Espergesia" (138) this anguish makes him feel not only stranded in an absurd world but estranged from his fellow men. This situation he attributes to an accident of birth. He had the misfortune, he complains, to be born on a day when God was off colour and consequently botched up his creation:

> Yo nací un día
> que Dios estuvo enfermo.

As a result he has been born with a morbid sensitivity which denies him the spiritual health which others seem to enjoy and instead condemns him to suffer the malaise of one who can discover no meaning in life. Moreover, it is a malaise which he must suffer alone, for since most men live comfortable, complacent lives and understand only what they can see and touch, no one can probe the gaping wound he carries inside him, the void created in his soul by his loss of faith in life:

> Hay un vacío

> en mi aire metafísico
> que nadie ha de palpar.

Nor are others able to understand the anguish which permeates his poetry:

> Todos saben que vivo,
> que mastico . . . Y no saben
> por qué en mi verso chirrian,
> oscuro sinsabor de féretro,
> luyidos vientos
> desenroscados de la Esfinge
> preguntona del Desierto.

The Sphinx — a symbol inherited from Darío and the Modernists — represents the inscrutable enigma of life which is the source of the poet's anguish. For, unable to discover any meaningful explanation of existence on earth, he is nagged by the uneasy suspicion that death is all that lies at the end of it. The last stanza, bringing the poem back to its starting point, shows him trapped in the vicious circle of his malaise:

> Yo nací un día
> que Dios estuvo enfermo,
> grave.

The final punch-line not only underlines the gravity of his condition but also introduces a new element. The refrain, which builds up a sense of the fatality which dogs him, also echoes through the poem like a death knell. His malaise, it now becomes clear, is due not only to the morbid sensitivity inflicted on him at birth, but to his misfortune in being born at a time when God was sick and dying. For the modern world is one in which God is dead, a world where God no longer has any place since men have lost faith in traditional interpretations of the universe. The poet's anguish is born of that crisis.

It is noticeable, however, that Vallejo's view of the human condition tends to be very much coloured by his own personal sense of inadequacy. In *Los heraldos negros* his own childish helplessness is shared by a humanity abandoned by God to its own resources, and in one poem he accuses the Deity of being insensitive to the suffering of the creatures he has irresponsibly brought into being:

> Dios mío, si tú hubieras sido hombre,
> hoy supieras ser Dios;
> pero tú, que estuviste siempre bien,
> no sientes nada de tu creación.
> Y el hombre sí te sufre: el Dios es él!   (122)

More frequently, however, God is seen in the image of man, as a kindly, well-intentioned father who is just not up to the job of governing the universe, since he is as impotent as humanity in the face of an implacable destiny. "La de a mil" (109) compares him to the ragged lottery-ticket vendor whose title of *suertero* (bringer of luck) is a purely nominal one:

> Pasa el suertero que atesora, acaso
> nominal, como Dios,
> entre panes tantálicos, humana
> impotencia de amor.

Though the *suertero* might give us our heart's desire, he has no control over the lottery and is unable to bestow good fortune where he wishes. Behind the few prizes with which he tantalises us, he has a much greater store of disappointments caused by his powerlessness to convert his good wishes into reality. In like manner God is powerless to bend destiny to his will and defrauds man's expectations by holding out a tantalising prospect of spiritual fulfilment which he is never able to realise. God in name only, he is unable to live up to man's image of him, for despite his love of his children, he is powerless to lavish his blessings on them and so satisfy their spiritual hunger. Given this divine impotence, destiny operates of its own accord, in a fortuitous, haphazard way, uncontrolled by any supernatural agency, so that life becomes a mere lottery, a game of chance in which the odds are weighed heavily against man whose attempts to dodge the blows which are gratuitously aimed at him are to no avail since one of them must eventually hit the mark. Man, therefore, goes through life with the uneasiness of a panic-stricken criminal who knows that sooner or later he will be apprehended and punished, and when his turn comes to suffer the blows of fate, he accepts it resignedly as his due for having escaped so long unscathed, as if it were a crime to live and not to suffer:

> Y el hombre . . . Pobre . . . pobre! Vuelve los ojos, como
> cuando por sobre el hombro nos llama una palmada;
> vuelve los ojos locos, y todo lo vivido
> se empoza, como charco de culpa, en la mirada. (51)

Vallejo's unsatisfied longing for something which will give life a meaning and make it worth living often expresses itself, as in Beckett's *Waiting for Godot*, in the theme of an endless waiting for something to turn up which will transform existence. "La cena miserable" (116) is dominated by a note of impatient weariness. The poet has grown tired of waiting for something more than the mere existence which, it seems, is all the human condition entitles us to, and of being tantalised by the prospect of a salvation that always remains unattainable:

> Hasta cuándo estaremos esperando lo que
> no se nos debe . . . Y en qué recodo estiraremos
> nuestra pobre rodilla para siempre! Hasta cuándo

la cruz que nos alienta no detendrá sus remos.

The cross before which he kneels recedes from him like a carrot dangling in front of a donkey, so that life is a pilgrimage on his knees, an unending journey leading nowhere, and he longs for the turn in the road where he might at last rest in peace. A long-suffering and much decorated veteran of the army of the doubtful, he is weary of soldiering on without the comfort of some absolute, some certainty in which to believe:

Hasta cuándo la Duda nos brindará blasones
por haber padecido . . .

In characteristic fashion Vallejo goes on to express his unsatisfied metaphysical longings in elemental terms, as the privation of the basic creature comforts of warmth, nourishment, affection, companionship. The human condition is likened to that of a child who has woken up in the night crying with hunger and sits alone in the darkness endlessly waiting at table for the light of morning when he can eat his fill in company with the rest of the family:

Ya nos hemos sentado
mucho a la mesa, con la amargura de un niño
que a media noche, llora de hambre, desvelado . . .

Y cuando nos veremos con los demás, al borde
de una mañana eterna, desayunados todos.

Weary of the meagre, unsatisfying supper that is his lot on earth, the poet looks forward to death which, if it does not guarantee him a state of bliss in an after-life, at least represents a release from the miseries and frustrations of this world. But, like a drunkard, the dark force of destiny — which, using the black spoon of the grave to devour humanity, is the one well-fed individual in a hungry world — toys with man, dangling death tantalisingly before his eyes only to snatch it away again:

Hay alguien que ha bebido mucho, y se burla,
y acerca y aleja de nosotros, como negra cuchara
de amarga esencia humana, la tumba . . .
Y menos sabe
ese oscuro hasta cuándo la cena durará!

Operating capriciously, even destiny does not know when it will strike to bring an individual's miserable existence to an end, and the poet has no alternative but to go on living and suffering in a world whose senseless absurdity manifests itself in the whimsical workings of fate.

Thus the doctrines in which Vallejo was brought up simply do not correspond to his experience of the world. In "Trilce XII" (154) the arbitrary nature of a life where misfortune strikes capriciously seems to him to make nonsense of all concepts of a rationally ordered universe:

> Chasquido de moscón que muere
> a mitad de su vuelo y cae a tierra.
> ¿Qué dice ahora Newton?

In one of the compositions from *Poemas humanos* the senseless absurdity he sees around him indicates that God's grand design exists only in the head of the Deity if it exists at all:

> Un disparate ... En tanto,
> es así, más acá de la cabeza de Dios.   (411)

Hence the poet is confronted by a reality with which his mind is unable to cope. In "Los heraldos negros" (51), he reacts with confused bewilderment to the gratuitous cruelty of life, shaking his head disbelievingly at the hardness of its blows, unable to understand or explain why they should befall him:

> Hay golpes en la vida, tan fuertes ... Yo no sé!
> Golpes como del odio de Dios; como si ante ellos,
> la resaca de todo lo sufrido
> se empozara en el alma ... Yo no sé!

Later, in *Poemas humanos*, he is no nearer to understanding why life is so cruel nor why he was born so ill-equipped to cope with it. The best he can do is to laugh off his anguish with wry humour. Having been granted the gift of life, he ironically chides himself, he ought not to be so ungrateful as to expect to understand it as well:

> Que saber por qué tiene la vida este perrazo,
> por qué lloro, por qué,
> cejón, inhábil, veleidoso, hube nacido
> gritando;
> saberlo, comprenderlo
> al son de un alfabeto competente,
> sería padecer por un ingrato.   (393)

In the lines from "Los heraldos negros" quoted above, not only is Vallejo unable to explain why he should suffer life's blows, but he cannot find words capable of expressing the pain they inflict and his attempts to do so taper off in a confession of hopeless inadequacy. Just as traditional doctrines do not correspond to his experience of life and reason does not enable him to understand it, so, too, the language he has inherited does not equip him to define that experience. Again and again he is confronted by the inadequacy of the materials of his craft to the point where his very pen fails him when he tries to write:

> Y hasta la misma pluma
> con que escribo por último se troncha.   (174)

In "Intensidad y altura" (347) he attributes his failure to give poetic expression to his experience to the fact that he must employ a medium which is not designed to communicate the raw material of experience but to reduce it to manageable, comprehensible proportions:

> Quiero escribir, pero me sale espuma,
> quiero decir muchísmo y me atollo;
> no hay cifra hablada que no sea suma,
> no hay pirámide escrita, sin cogollo.

> Quiero escribir, pero me siento puma;
> quiero laurearme, pero me encebollo.
> No hay toz hablada, que no llegue a bruma,
> no hay dios ni hijo de dios, sin desarrollo.

Traditionally a poem is a linguistic structure which condenses multifarious reality and organises it into a coherent entity. But the immediate, elemental experience which the poet wishes to communicate ("me siento puma", "me encebollo") cannot be conveyed in this manner, for as soon as the original experience is translated into words, as soon as the cough begins to be voiced ("toz"), it is dissipated and, subject to the universal law of evolution, develops into something different. Hence Vallejo aspires to write with his ear, to express his experience directly, unadulterated by poetic elaboration:

> Oh no cantar; apenas
> escribir y escribir con un palito
> o con el filo de la oreja inquieta! (387)

Though, of course, such an ambition is impossible to achieve, it does indicate what Vallejo is aiming at in his poetry. The disconcerting syntax and linguistic contortions of *Trilce* and *Poemas humanos* represent an attempt to develop a personal language which will faithfully express his experience of reality, a language which will enable him to define that experience and thereby come to terms with it. It is through poetry that Vallejo strives to cope with a reality which is beyond his rational comprehension.

Vallejo's fundamental inability to cope with life persists into the later poetry of *Poemas humanos*. As a South American exile in Paris, he experienced the same loneliness and insecurity as in Lima, aggravated now by the rigours of the European climate, his precarious economic situation and illness, and he was prone to moods of black despondency, as in "Piedra negra sobre una piedra blanca" (341):

> Me moriré en París con aguacero,
> un día del cual tengo ya el recuerdo.
> Me moriré en París — y no me corro —
> talvez un jueves, como es hoy, de otoño.

> Jueves será, porque hoy, jueves, que proso
> estos versos, los húmeros me he puesto
> a la mala y, jamás como hoy, me he vuelto,
> con todo mi camino, a verme solo.

On his travels through life, he complains, he has never been so completely alone as he is now in the great, impersonal city of Paris. Depressed by the falling rain, the approaching winter and the humdrum of day-to-day life, he feels that nothing will go right for him — the verses he tries to compose turn out to be mere prose and his forearms begin to ache as irritation spreads through his body — and that everyone and everything is against him. Thoroughly disheartened, he foresees that his death will take place on a day like today. Paradoxically, he refers to it as something which he has already experienced. For this dreary day reflects the pattern of his whole existence, it is but one of a succession of such days which are slowly destroying him, and he is too dispirited even to want to evade the death they have in store for him. No nearer to coping now than he was in *Trilce*, he can do no more than protest, like a defenceless child unjustly punished, against the world's victimisation of him:

> César Vallejo ha muerto, le pegaban
> todos sin que él les haga nada;
> le daban duro con un palo y duro
> también con una soga . . .

In *Trilce* Vallejo found in the walls of his prison cell a concrete symbol for the limitations imposed on him by a world which thwarted his aspirations to a full and satisfying life. In *Poemas humanos* those limitations assume dingy material form in the trivia of the dull day-to-day routine with which his straitened circumstances made him all too familiar. Now his prison is the house where he is trapped by the domestic routine, repeating the same inconsequential acts day after day in an endless cycle of futility:

> Ello es que el lugar donde me pongo
> el pantalón, es una casa donde
> me quito la camisa en alta voz . . .   (433)

The repeated frustration of the poet's deepest longings, the contradiction between his inner vision of what life ought to be and the drab reality of what it is, leads him to view existence as an absurdity. If, after all his striving for transcendence, he is to succumb to the soul-destroying, humdrum routine of day-to-day life, if the stars are beyond his reach and he must live surrounded by combs and dirty handkerchiefs, then life is hardly worth living and it would be best if it came to an end:

¡Y si después de tanta historia, sucumbimos,
no ya de eternidad,
sino de esas cosas sencillas, como estar
en la casa o ponerse a cavilar!
¡Y si luego encontramos,
de buenas a primeras, que vivimos,
a juzgar por la altura de los astros,
por el peine y las manchas del pañuelo!
¡Más valdría, en verdad,
que se lo coman todo, desde luego! (371)

With a weary sense of frustration which is often disguised by a self-deprecating irony, Vallejo observes the gulf between aspiration and reality in the duality of his own being. For while his spirit holds up to him a vision of a higher life, his experience of hunger and illness brings home to him the extent to which his existence is lived on an elemental level, through that frail, decaying body of his which constantly demands satisfaction of its appetites and repeatedly breaks down under the effects of illness and age.[4] "Epístola a los transeúntes" (293) describes his daily life as the elemental routine of an animal. Each morning he goes out fearfully to engage in the daily struggle for survival, cowering before the world like a hunted rabbit, and at night he returns to the safety of his burrow to relax with the bloated contentment of a sleeping elephant:

Reanudo mi día de conejo,
mi noche de elefante en descanso.

Mimicking Christ's words at the Last Supper — "... this is my body ... this is my blood" (Mark 14.22-24) — to underline ironically the distance between the latter's divinity and his own animality, he surveys his body like a mechanic inspecting a machine which will not respond to the controls:

ésta es mi inmensidad en bruto, a cántaros,
éste es mi grato peso, que me buscara abajo para pájaro;
éste es mi brazo
que por su cuenta rehusó ser ala ...
éste ... mi estómago en que cupo mi lámpara en pedazos.

Though he is aware of the attractions of the flesh and is only too willing to partake of its pleasures, he feels completely dominated by the

4. Jean Franco (*César Vallejo. The Dialectics of Poetry and Silence*. [Cambridge: Cambridge Univ. Press, 1976]) points out that a crucial factor in the spiritual crisis of the young Vallejo was the impact of evolutionist theory as popularised by Ernst Haeckel, which led him to the conclusion that individual liberty is illusory since the individual is subject to the biological laws of the species. Now, in middle age, he seems to see those theories confirmed by his own experience.

immense mass of his body, which seems to have a will of its own, its own idea of what is good for him. It condescends to give the inner man temporary liberation via its own lower regions, to afford him momentary fulfilment through sex, but it insists on remaining firmly anchored to the ground and steadfastly refuses to raise him to the heights of a spiritually satisfying existence. His stomach, insatiable in its demands for feeding, ends up by devouring the lamp of his ideals. Again and again *Poemas humanos* insists on the frustration of the poet's spiritual aspirations by the limitations of the flesh. Though his imagination is able to roam free beyond all earthly bounds, he can never reach the realms it so tantalisingly reveals to him, for he is held prisoner by a body too strong for him to subjugate:

> y cautivo en tu enorme libertad,
> arrastrado por tu hércules autónomo . . .   (421)

Like a wild horse the body resists the soul's attempts to tame it and ends by up throwing the soul to the ground and placing it in a halter:

> Tú sabes lo que te duele,
> lo que te salta al anca,
> lo que baja por ti con soga al suelo . . .   (421)

Alongside these personal experiences, Vallejo's later poetry also reflects another collective crisis. In the uncertain political and economic climate of Europe in the 1920s and 1930s he witnessed what to him and many of his contemporaries seemed to be the death throes of Western civilisation. Thus, in "Los nueve monstruos" (321) his personal inability to cope is now shared by mankind in general. As man loses control of his world, the poet sees the floodgates burst open and suffering and misery spread with nightmarish rapidity:

> Y desgraciadamente,
> el dolor crece en el mundo a cada rato,
> crece a treinta minutos por segundo, paso a paso . . .

> Crece la desdicha, hermanos hombres,
> más pronto que la máquina, a diez máquinas, y crece
> con la res de Rousseau, con nuestras barbas;
> crece el mal por razones que ignoramos
> y es una inundación con propios líquidos,
> con propio barro y propia nube sólida!

Like a self-generating flood, evil seems to propagate of its own accord, outstripping man's capacity to combat it and exposing the inadequacies of industrialised society and the liberal, democratic state, the *res publica* that was the sacred cow of Rousseau and other thinkers of the Enlightenment. Unchecked, evil turns a once-ordered world on its head, reducing it to chaos:

> Invierte el sufrimiento posiciones, da función
> en que el humor acuoso es vertical
> al pavimento,
> el ojo es visto y esta oreja oída,
> y esta oreja da nueve campanadas a la hora
> del rayo, y nueve carcajadas
> a la hora del trigo, y nueve sones hembras
> a la hora del llanto, y nueve cánticos
> a la hora del hambre, y nueve truenos
> y nueve látigos, menos un grito.

In men's reaction to the misfortunes loosed on them like biblical plagues, the thing most conspicuously missing is the virile cry of rebellion and self-assertion. Instead humanity resigns itself with feminine passiveness, lamenting, giving way to hysteria, offering up prayers to God, or bringing fresh misfortunes on its head by embracing order in the form of strident and brutal Fascist authoritarianism ("nueve truenos/y nueve látigos"). Clearly there is a need for decisive action, and the poet turns inquiringly to the political authorities:

> Señor Ministro de Salud: ¿qué hacer?
> ¡Ah! desgraciadamente, hombres humanos,
> hay, hermanos, muchísimo que hacer.

The question, however, is a rhetorical one, for it is evident that the existing socio-political apparatus is incapable of containing the spread of evil. The poem, therefore, ends with a sigh and a recognition of the immensity of the task which confronts man before he can re-establish his control over the world.

In his own failing health Vallejo saw an image of the human condition and in "El alma que sufrió de ser su cuerpo" (421) he assumes the role of a doctor diagnosing the sickness of an ailing humanity:

> Tú sufres de una glándula endocrínica, se ve,
> o, quizá,
> sufres de mí, de mi sagacidad escueta, tácita.

The frailty and imperfection of the body condemn the human animal to physical suffering, but much more serious, the poet-doctor insinuates, is the malaise brought on by reasoning which, by destroying illusions and laying bare the vanity of things, insidiously undermines his spiritual health. Since man is unable to find any meaning to life, he has no real existence and lives only through the anguished sense of futility which is slowly destroying him and which has become contagious in an age when all human values seem to have failed:

> Tú, pobre hombre, vives; no lo niegues,
> si mueres; no lo niegues,
> si mueres de tu edad ¡ay! y de tu época.

The only certainty in man's life is that he has been born into a world where he does not feel at home and where he sees no alternative but to endure his lot of suffering with stoic resignation. Still bearing the scar left by the traumatic experience of birth, he contemplates his navel with anguished bewilderment, unable to understand how he came to be cast adrift in this disconcerting and alien world or why he should have been born at all:

> Tú, luego, has nacido; eso
> también se ve de lejos, infeliz y cállate,
> y soportas la calle que te dio la suerte,
> a tu ombligo interrogas: ¿dónde? ¿cómo?

His limited reasoning powers are insufficient to show him a way out of his dilemma and, indeed, only aggravate his torment, for his painful mental efforts keep bringing him face to face with the dual nature of his existence, the contradiction between his inner vision of what life ought to be and the objective reality of what it is:

> Pero si tú calculas en tus dedos hasta dos,
> es peor; no lo niegues, hermanito.

Not only does man seem incapable of remedying his condition by himself, but he prefers to delude himself rather than to recognise its gravity. Hence he rejects the poet-doctor's diagnosis, and the latter brings the consultation to a close by ironically wishing the patient the good health to continue suffering:

> ¡Salud! ¡Y sufre!

"La rueda del hambriento" (361), a poem set against the background of the Depression, expresses through the persona of a starving beggar not only the plight of the unemployed masses but that of a humanity whose traditional values have failed it. The beggar's pleas for a stone on which to rest and bread to appease his hunger go unanswered and he is left alone to brood on his destitution:

> Una piedra en qué sentarme
> ¿no habrá ahora para mí? . . .
> Un pedazo de pan, ¿tampoco habrá ahora para mí? . . .
> pero dadme
> en español
> algo, en fin, de beber, de comer, de vivir, de reposarse,
> y después me iré . . .
> Hallo una extraña forma, está muy rota
> y sucia mi camisa
> y ya no tengo nada, esto es horrendo.

Parodying the Lord's Prayer and St. Matthew's Gospel — "Everyone that asks, will receive . . ." (7.8-11) —, the poem is both an ironic comment on the death of God in the modern world and an expression of humanity's hunger for a new faith which would nourish it emotionally, provide a solid basis for existence and incorporate the alienated individual (the beggar) into a united human family.

In a sense Vallejo's conversion to Marxism provided him with the faith he was looking for. "Los nueve monstruos" and "El alma que sufrió de ser su cuerpo" are both written from a Marxist viewpoint, the underlying implication being that Marxism holds the solution to the evils of the world and the spiritual illness of modern man. Yet the latter is a contradictory poem. On one level it is to be read as a dialogue between the poet and his alter ego, and the religious connotations of the title indicate that Vallejo was unable to free himself from metaphysical needs which a materialistic doctrine like Marxism could never satisfy. At the end of the poem the poet-patient rejects the diagnosis of the poet-doctor and, by implication, the Marxist remedy which would cure his sickness. There is thus a genuine conflict within the poet as he feels himself torn in two different directions at once. In the persona of the doctor he disapproves of his own metaphysical preoccupations as an expression of decadent bourgeois individualism, but at the same time, in the persona of the patient, he experiences a metaphysical anguish of which no amount of reasoning can rid him. This anguish was to become more acute as Vallejo felt life begin to slip away from him and "Un pilar soportando consuelos . . ." (351) presents an ironic picture of a Marxist desperately turning to religion for comfort as he is seized by panic at the prospect of death. A dramatisation of the poet's state of mind, the poem shows him on his knees in a church whose pillars stand as a symbol of the moral support which religion offers to those who are about to pass through the dark door of death:

> Un pilar soportando consuelos,
> pilar otro,
> pilar en duplicado, pilaroso
> y como nieto de una puerta oscura.

Though the weary, disillusioned side of his personality looks on sceptically and dismisses prayer as a waste of breath, his thirst for immortality beyond the grave leads him to drink greedily from the chalice of hope:

> Ruido perdido, el uno, oyendo, al borde del cansancio;
> bebiendo, el otro, dos a dos, con asas.

In the end he is too honest to delude himself and recognises that the only liberation from the terror of death lies in death itself, but, together with a whole series of compositions from his final volume, the poem furnishes clear evidence that Marxism did not enable Vallejo to come to terms with his personal anguish.

Hence it is not surprising that, while he admired the party militants who devoted themselves body and soul to the creation of a Socialist utopia, he should feel himself incapable of such total commitment. Thus, in "Salutación angélica" (291), after placing the Russian Bolshevik on a pedestal as the embodiment of Socialist virtues, he confesses his inability to match his revolutionary dedication. There is nothing he would like better, he protests, than to share the Bolshevik's fervour for the coldly rational and solidly based doctrines of Marxism and with him to march unhesitatingly and inexorably forward towards the brave new world of the future:

> Yo quisiera, por eso,
> tu calor doctrinal, frío y en barras,
> tu añadida manera de mirarnos
> y aquesos tuyos pasos metalúrgicos,
> aquesos tuyos pasos de otra vida.

But the truth is, he confesses, that he is but a mere mortal dwarfed by the Bolshevik's almost inhuman greatness and subject to ordinary human weaknesses, and within him there lurks a doubting alter ego which prevents him from seeing things with clear-sighted vision and keeps him from answering the Bolshevik's call and following in his footsteps:

> Y digo, bolchevique, tomando esta flaqueza
> en su feroz linaje de exhalación terrestre;
> hijo natural del bien y del mal
> y viviendo tal vez por vanidad, para que digan,
> me dan tus simultáneas estaturas mucha pena,
> puesto que tú no ignoras en quién se me hace tarde diaria-
> mente,
> en quién estoy callado y medio tuerto.

The tone of these stanzas is ambivalent. Vallejo experiences a sense of guilt, for he genuinely admires the Bolshevik's subordination of self to the collective cause, but he is aware that he is too old a dog to learn new tricks and to suppress doubts and self-questionings and he cannot resist poking irony at his hero's single-minded commitment. There is no trace of irony, however, in "Himno a los voluntarios de la República" (439), where he is cast in the role of spectator lost in admiration for the heroics of the militiamen of the Spanish Republic:

> Voluntario de España, miliciano
> de huesos fidedignos, cuando marcha a morir tu corazón,
> cuando marcha a matar con su agonía
> mundial, no sé verdaderamente
> qué hacer, dónde ponerme . . .

He is assailed by guilt and inferiority as he, the vacillating intellectual, stands idly on the side-lines while workers and peasants put their lives at risk to build a new world. Incapable of advancing into the future with this new breed of men who think and act in collective terms, he feels that he is doomed to lag behind them as a sorry relic of the stone-age of bourgeois individualism:

> desde mi piedra en blanco, déjame,
> solo,
> cuadrumano, más acá, mucho más lejos,
> al no caber entre mis manos tu largo rato extático,
> quiebro contra tu rapidez de doble filo
> mi pequeñez en traje de grandeza!

Yet, however unworthy Vallejo felt himself to be in comparison with the Bolshevik and the militiamen, he was drawn to Marxism not only by his personal need for a faith but by a genuine concern for the underprivileged. A constant feature of his poetry is a compassionate awareness of and a guilt-ridden sense of responsibility for the suffering of others. Thus, as he sits breakfasting, in one of his early poems, his mind drifts to the starving wretches in the cold world outside and he is tormented by the thought that by consuming this repast he is depriving some poor unfortunate of the means of staying alive. His whole existence, he feels, is lived at someone else's expense:

> Todos mis huesos son ajenos;
> yo talvez los robé!
> Yo vine a darme lo que acaso estuvo
> asignado para otro;
> y pienso que, si no hubiera nacido,
> otro pobre tomara este café!
> Yo soy un mal ladrón . . . A dónde iré!   (110)

These feelings were heightened by the widespread misery which Vallejo witnessed in Europe during the Depression and poems like "La rueda del hambriento" (361) and "Parado en una piedra . . ." (335) express his horror and indignation at the plight of the destitute unemployed. However, Marxism did not come easily to Vallejo, for, despite his emotional identification with his fellows, he had a jaundiced view of human nature which made it difficult for him to believe that man was capable of improving his lot. These conflicting attitudes come into opposition in "Considerando en frío . . ." (329) where the poet, in the manner of a prosecuting attorney, coldly analyses the human condition and accumulates evidence to prove to himself that man is a miserable creature beyond redemption. Man, he remarks disdainfully, "es lóbrego mamífero y se peina", he is an animal whose tendency to brood and social refinements grotesquely emphasise his basic animality. He is an animal who on occasion laboriously ponders his unhappy condition, but more often he shuts his mind to the thought that he lives under the threat of death and that at any moment he is liable to be stretched out like an inanimate object, and contrives to achieve an illusion of happiness in an unconscious, unthinking routine:

> ... el hombre se queda, a veces, pensando,
> como queriendo llorar,
> y sujeto a tenderse como objeto,
> se hace buen carpintero, suda, mata,
> y luego, canta, almuerza, se abotona ...

After such a devastating exposition of man's failings, the logical conclusion would be for the poet to wash his hands of him and retreat into misanthropic isolation. Instead Vallejo is overcome by tenderness. Calling the human animal over to him, he hugs him in a fraternal embrace, and though reason tells him that he should know better, he shrugs off his shame-faced embarrassment and gives way to his feelings:

> le hago una seña,
> viene,
> y le doy un abrazo, emocionado.
> ¡Qué más da! Emocionado ... Emocionado ...

In the end, therefore, Vallejo's instinctive solidarity with his fellows and an emotional need to believe in man were to triumph over his scepticism, and in the figures of the Russian Bolshevik and the Spanish militiaman he saw evidence that men were indeed capable of changing their nature, of transcending the egoism of centuries to work together in fraternity to build a better world. Thus, while he was realistic enough to recognise that Marxism could not resolve his own personal existential predicament, he was convinced that it did offer a long-term solution to the ills of mankind. There was no limit, it seemed to him, to what a united humanity would be capable of achieving, and in the "Himno a los voluntarios de la República" (443) he draws his inspiration from the Bible to prophesy a future Socialist paradise where all evil will have been abolished:

> ¡Entrelazándose hablarán los mudos, los tullidos andarán!
> ¡Verán, ya de regreso, los ciegos
> y palpitando escucharán los sordos! ...
> ¡Sólo la muerte morirá!

He was aware, of course, that he himself would not live to see that brave new world come into being. Nonetheless, the belief that his newly-found faith would one day redeem the species gave a meaning and purpose to his individual existence and helped to sustain him through the personal anguish of his later years.

However, Vallejo's political optimism was to suffer a severe buffeting as the revolutionary movement was crushed in China and then in Spain and the Russian Revolution lapsed into Stalinist Terror.[5] "Al revés de las aves ..." (429) records the euphoric mood of the 1920s and 1930s, when Revolution seemed to be ushering in a new era for mankind, and the bitter disappointment caused by subsequent events, which seemed to confirm the jaundiced view that humanity would never change and was beyond redemption:

> ... fuera entonces
> que vi que el hombre es mal nacido,
> mal vivo, mal muerto, mal moribundo.

On this occasion the poet's stomach churns over with frustration and impotent rage:

> Todo esto
> agítase, ahora mismo,
> en mi vientre de macho extrañamente.

On other occasions the thwarting of the cause in which he had placed all his hope and faith leads him to succumb to despair. Thus, as he prepares to go to his death in "Despedida recordando un adiós" (375), he has nothing to bequeath to humanity but a legacy of frustrated ideals, among which is "este sueño práctico del alma", his dream of a world transformed by love in action in the form of Socialism, a dream which has proved to be his "último vaso de humo", his last cup of disappointment. The world of which he takes his leave is one which seems to him to be collapsing into chaos, an absurd world where Marxism has been no more successful in establishing a meaningful order than any other religious, philosophical or political system devised by man:

> Adiós, hermanos san pedros,
> heráclitos, erasmos, espinozas!
> Adiós, tristes obispos bolcheviques!
> Adiós, gobernadores en desorden!

The final image that emerges of Vallejo is of a man who, as defeat and death stare him in the face, clings desperately to a belief in the ultimate and inevitable triumph of Socialism. Reluctantly recognising that the attempt to build in Spain a new society which would be a mother to the masses is doomed to fail, he urges those who survive him to continue working and struggling to make it a reality:

5. R.K. Britton ("The political dimension of César Vallejo's *Poemas humanos*", *Modern Language Review*, LXX, 3 [1975], 539-49) shows that the poem "Otro poco de calma, camarada" is addressed to Stalin and voices Vallejo's misgivings about the course the Revolution was taking under his leadership.

> ... si la madre
> España cae — digo, es un decir —
> salid, niños del mundo; id a buscarla! ...   (479)

3

CARLOS GERMAN BELLI

The originality of Carlos Germán Belli (b. 1927) lies in his development of a personal style which combines elements derived from Spanish poetry of the Golden Age – a classical or archaic vocabulary; a disconcerting syntax characterised by hyberbaton and ellipsis; the frequent use of reiterative epithets; a predilection for the hendecasyllable and the heptasyllable – with contemporary themes and modern and colloquial language and imagery.[1] In contrast to Vallejo, whose travels uprooted him from his native soil and cast him adrift in a large and alien world, Belli expresses in his work the alienation and frustration of a man who does not feel at home in the narrow and familiar confines of his native city. In "Cepo de Lima" (87) he describes himself as a man defeated and demoralised and attributes the blame to Lima. Those who have had the misfortune to be born in the Peruvian capital, he complains, are caught in a trap which inexorably crushes and destroys them:

> Por tu cepo es, ¡ay Lima!, bien lo sé,
> que tanto cuna cuanto tumba es siempre
> para quien acá nace, vive y muere.

Early in the same poem he offers us a self-portrait in which he walks among the rubble of his ruined body with the fleshless skin hanging down from his neck like the crest of a cock with its throat cut:

---

1. Belli's first books, *Poemas* (1958) and *Dentro & Fuera* (1960), show a marked influence of Surrealism and other avant-garde movements, the result of his reading of Tzara, Breton and Michaux among others. *¡Oh Hada Cibernética!* (1961) initiates an evolution towards an original expression and in *El pie sobre el cuello* (1964) and *Por el monte abajo* (1966) Belli arrives at artistic maturity, an evolution which coincides with a growing interest in Spanish classical poets, mainly Herrera, Medrano, Góngora, Francisco de la Torre and Francisco de Rioja. These five collections are gathered together in *El pie sobre el cuello* (Montevideo: Alfa, 1967). Unless otherwise indicated, all references are to this text. Subsequently Belli has published *Sextinas y otros poemas* (Santiago de Chile: Universitaria, 1970) and *¡Oh Hada Cibernética!* (Caracas: Monte Avila, 1971). The latter is an anthology, but includes a new collection entitled *El libro de los nones*.

> Como cresta de gallo acuchillado,
> un largo granulado pellejuelo,
> de la garganta pende con exceso;
>
> y por debajo de las ambas patas,
> cascotes no de yeso, mas de carne,
> como mustios escombros de una casa.

These stanzas illustrate a tendency to wallow in imagery of hyperbolic horror and to translate spiritual suffering into physical terms, so that demoralisation in face of life is presented as a disintegration of the body. Behind this would seem to lie a concept of poetry as a kind of personal catharsis, a means by which the poet purges himself of the pain that life causes him. As was the case with Vallejo, it is ultimately through poetry that Belli comes to terms with life.

A government employee, Belli gives voice to the humiliations and frustrations of the office-worker caught in the daily grind of a dull, soul-destroying job which earns him barely enough to support his family; whose circumstances deny him the possibility of fulfilling himself as a human being; who sees before him no prospect but a life-time of unrewarding and demoralising toil. With characteristic hyperbole he depicts work as a state of cruel servitude which strips him of his human dignity and reduces him to the level of a beast of burden:

> y en horma yo lucía de cuadrúpedo,
> del hocico a la cola,
> exactamente un bruto.   (89)

Poems like "Los bofes" (75) translate bureaucratic drudgery into images of physical strain and exhaustion. The opening line juxtaposes the colloquialism "botar bofes" with a classical hyperbaton that could have been taken straight from Góngora, and the incongruity between the majestic turn of phrase and the idea it expresses underlines the poet's humiliating, slave-like condition:

> Estos que hoy bofes boto mal mi grado,
> tamaños montes cuando me jubile,
> como mil dejaré al fin (¡ja, ja, ja!
> bofes, ¡ja, ja, ja! bofes nunca más);
> y redimido así de bofes ya
> hacia la huesa iré con talares alas,
> antes que tornen mala vez de nuevo
> amos viles a donde mí con priesa,
> a llenarme el vacío cuerpo y liso,
> para que luego luego, mal mi grado,
> bote yo otras mil nuevas asaduras.

The effectiveness of these lines derives primarily from the use of a figurative expression in a literal sense: the poet has spewed his guts out so much in labour that by the time he retires he will have left mountains of them and his body will be emptied of its entrails. However, his gleeful chortling over the prospect of future freedom immediately gives way to the uneasy suspicion that his masters are capable of stuffing his entrails back into his body so that he can go on slogging his guts out for them. Only in death, he concludes, can he be sure of finally freeing himself from his toils.

In the manner of the impotent slave he feels himself to be, Belli takes his revenge with the only weapon available to him: his imagination. In "Ras con ras" (90) he savours with sadistic pleasure a vision of what death will mean for his masters. The great leveller will reduce everyone to equality and the corpses of the mighty, like those of the humble, will serve as food for the "delicate stomachs" of the elements:

> Los cuerpos en la tumba parejos al fin yacen,
> y a pulpa reducidos, rallados, machacados
> y en jalea aun trocados ídem por ídem ya,
> para los delicados estómagos del aire.

The poet's vengeful fantasy elaborates this vision and he revels in the thought that death will be a hell where the masters, tyrannised by the elements, will sweat eternally to provide them with food and will thus experience at first hand the enslavement to which they subjected their subordinates on earth:

> Pues los jefes hoy día, inmóviles ayer,
> gordas gotas rebosan en las arcas del éter,
> igual a trompicones de acá para acullá,
> y en el vivo retrato de sus subordinados
> para siempre trocándose bajo el talón del aire.

Other poems describe the hardship of struggling to make ends meet on an inadequate salary. As a reward for his labours the poet receives only crumbs, as if he and his family were ants instead of human beings ("Fisco", 97), and he prostrates himself at the feet of his daughters, ashamed at his failure to fulfil his responsibilities as a father ("Amanuense", 80). In the daily struggle to provide for his family he degrades himself, rooting like a pig among the scrub for a few ears of corn ("Sáficos adónicos", 88). On other occasions the struggle takes on an epic character. Since the world denies him sustenance, he goes beyond its bounds in a superhuman foraging expedition, sniffing in space for an atom of food or digging to the bowels of the earth for a few carbonised crumbs:

> no hay día que mi olfato no traspase
> los umbrales del suelo, el agua, el aire,
> a oliscar de ración siquiera un átomo

> para la boca de mis dos hijuelas,
> o descienda hasta el fuego impenetrable
> por unas migas ya carbonizadas.   (78)

In "El lucro, el lucro ..." (65) he wonders whether this incessant struggle to earn sustenance will end with death:

> ¿El lucro, el lucro al fin
> del reparador alimento habré,
> no del combustible orbe, mas del aire,
> ¡ay!, en seguida de que yo perezca,
> luego luego de aquestos fieros duelos?

The poem, however, leaves the question in doubt and insinuates the frightful possibility that his spirit will continue to undergo the privations which now afflict his body. Constantly beset by economic difficulties, the poet comes to speculate that the struggle for survival is an eternal cosmic law which will persist beyond the tomb.

Perhaps the major source of Belli's discontent is that the continuous demands of the daily struggle deprive him of the opportunity to lead a life of his own and to achieve personal fulfilment. Thus, "¡Oh alma mía empedrada ...!" (46) expresses the bitterness of a man who is resentful

> por no haber conocido el albedrío
> de disponer sus días
> durante todo el tiempo de la vida.

In many poems love stands as a symbol of the fulfilment for which the poet yearns and which his circumstances deny him. Love, like his salary, is doled out to him in meagre crumbs, he complains ("Cupido y Fisco", 103), and in "Sáficos adónicos" he looks back on

> ... mi florida edad, de Fili ajeno,
> por cuyo cuerpo y alma yo moría
>   siempre sediento.   (88)

The best years of his life have been wasted thirsting in vain for the woman of his dreams, and since he has no one to love him, he comes to feel that his existence is purposeless and that he is superfluous in the world:

> Qué hago con este aposento,
> este cuero,
> este seso,
> si nadie los codicia
> un poco.   (49)

Thus his failure to satisfy his need to love and be loved mirrors his failure to find an outlet for his inner potential and to fulfil himself as a man. The privation of love may be regarded, therefore, as a metaphor of the general frustration of his life.

That it is merely a poetic theme is a point which should be emphasised, for throughout his work the love of his wife and family is celebrated as the one positive force in his life. It is true that the outside world often impinges into the home to spoil the happiness he enjoys in the breast of his family. In "Amanuense" (80) he is tormented by guilt at not being able to provide his daughters with the decent standard of living they deserve, and in "Poema" (74) he accuses himself of egoism for bringing them into a world where they must suffer the same hardships that he has had to endure. "Poema" (91) begs his wife's forgiveness for the insensitivity with which he often responds to her love and attributes it to the brutalising effect of his constant humiliations. Elsewhere his tendency to brood on his woes casts a shadow over the home and in "Mis ajos" (102) it is described as a pestilent odour infecting the garden of his daughters' childhood:

Pero mal padre soy, varón tan loco,
porque el jardín cercano de mis hijas,
con mal olor de feos bulbos siempre
infesto todo.

Yet, in spite of everything, the home remains his one oasis of happiness in a world where he feels hounded. "A mi esposa" (89) pays tribute to his wife for redeeming him from his condition of brute beast and restoring to him his dignity as a man:

Mas vos llegasteis al pesebre mío
y mudado fui a vuestra afana grey,
por siempre recobrando
la faz y el seso humano.

In the face of his daughters he contemplates the light of the heavens for the first time ("La cara de mis hijas"[2]), and he feels himself protected by a coat of mail woven by them ("Poema", 75). In the love of his family and the responsibility he feels for them he finds the strength and courage to face the world and to struggle on without flinching:

pero no cejaré, no, aunque no escriba
ni copule ni baile en esta Bética
no bella, en donde tantos años vivo.   (67)

Underlying Belli's work is a view of the world similar in many ways to that of Vallejo, that of a cruelly competitive world where only the strong survive and in face of which he feels hopelessly inadequate. Like "Trilce XLVII", "Poema" (78) presents birth as a catastrophe and evokes the apprehension of the foetus as it reluctantly emerges from the shelter of the womb into a cold, alien world:

2.   *¡Oh Hada Cibernética!*, p.124.

> Frunce el feto su frente
> y sus cejas enarca cuando pasa
> del luminoso vientre
> al albergue terreno,
> do se truecan sin tasa
> la luz en niebla, la cisterna en cieno;
> y abandonar le duele al fin el claustro,
> en que no rugen ni cierzo ni austro.

The final lines, however, introduce an element not present in Vallejo's poem, adding, as a further reason for the foetus' apprehension, that after the trauma of birth it runs the risk of

> . . . verse aun despeñado
> desde el más alto risco,
> cual un feto no amado,
> por tartamudo o cojo o manco o bizco.

The image of the deformed baby dashed to death from a cliff-top implies that life is implacably cruel to the weak: those who are born with some defect are destined to suffer for it, so that not only does life place them at a disadvantage at the outset but later punishes them for the very deficiencies with which it has afflicted them.

In a series of poems Belli sees in the infirmity of his spastic brother Alfonso evidence of the fundamental injustice of life which capriciously favours some and discriminates against others. "A mi hermano Alfonso" (76) employs one of his favourite images — the trap — to symbolise the illness which immobilises his brother and roots him to the earth like an oyster:

> Pues tanto el leño cuanto el crudo hierro
> del cepo que severo te avasalla,
> unidos cual un órgano se encuentran
> desde el cuello hasta las plantas,
> no sólo a flor de cuero,
> mas sí en el lecho de tu propio tuétano,
> que te dejan cual ostra
> a la faz del orbe así arraigado;
> y el leve vuelo en fin
> que en el cerúleo claustro siempre ejerce
> el ave más que el austro desalada,
> ¿cuándo a ti llegará?,
> mientras abajo tú en un aprisco solo
> no mueves hueso alguno
> ni agitas ya la lengua
> para llamar al aire;
> pues en el orbe todo viene y va
> al soplo de la vida,
> que pródigo se torna

> para muchos y a no más otros pocos
> áspero, vano o nada para siempre.

Comparing Alfonso's paralysis to the liberty of the bird which flies at will through the skies, the poet protests against the injustice that the freedom of movement which is the breath of life should inexplicably be denied to a few unfortunates like his brother while being lavished on every other creature in the universe.

Far from attenuating the fundamental injustices of life, the society depicted in Belli's poetry reflects and accentuates them. In "Segregación No. 1" (15) Peru is seen, through the eyes of a child, as a country where the poor skulk underground while on the earth above a small privileged class owns everything, manages everything in its own interest and enjoys all the advantages of wealth and power:

> Yo, mamá, mis dos hermanos
> y muchos peruanitos
> abrimos un hueco hondo, hondo
> donde nos guarecemos,
> porque arriba todo tiene dueño,
> todo está cerrado con llave,
> sellado firmemente,
> porque arriba todo tiene reserva:
> la sombra del árbol, las flores,
> los frutos, el techo, las ruedas,
> el agua, los lápices,
> y optamos por hundirnos
> en el fondo de la tierra,
> más abajo que nunca,
> lejos muy lejos de los jefes,
> hoy domingo,
> lejos muy lejos de los dueños,
> entre las patas de los animalitos,
> porque arriba
> hay algunos que manejan todo,
> que escriben, que cantan, que bailan,
> que hablan hermosamente,
> y nosotros rojos de vergüenza,
> tan sólo deseamos desaparecer
> en pedacitititos.

The child explains that he and his kind have been driven underground because on the face of the earth everything belongs to others and there is no room for them; they have taken refuge there to escape the tyranny of their masters whose power extends everywhere; and, finally, they have burrowed into the ground to hide the shame of their poverty and vulgarity from the scornful eyes of the elegant, refined rich. This underground world is, therefore, a metaphor of the misery, oppression and humiliation which constitute the only inheritance of the poor. The effectiveness of the poem derives from the child's ingenuous inability to comprehend why the adult world should permit injustices and absurdities which he perceives so clearly. His aggrieved and helpless bewilderment is that of the poet himself.

Various poems establish a contrast between the hardships and frustrations enjoyed by the poet and the affluence and well-being enjoyed by the privileged. Thus, "Por el monte abajo" (104) voices his envy of those fortunate beings who, favoured by the advantages of their class, prosper without effort, as if the whole universe had been bestowed upon them by destiny that they might sate each and every one of their appetites:

> Cuán fácil otros van a más sin pena,
> centuplicando el todo así boyantes,
> como si dellos fuere el sino sólo
> el alma y cuerpo a tutiplén llenar
> con aire, fuego y agua.

In this poem the competitiveness of social life is conveyed through the metaphor of the mountain, at whose peak lies the prize of well-being, understood not only in terms of economic comfort but, above all, as a state of independence permitting the individual to fulfil himself as a human being. While the favoured few scale the heights with rapid ease, the poet, despite his struggles to rise, goes slithering downhill to end up in the derisory subterranean kingdom that is the humiliating inheritance of the poor:

> En tanto que los otros raudo suben,
> a la par a este feudo nos venimos,
> a derribarnos en sus hondos antros
> que así tal vez el horroroso cetro
> del deterioro habremos.

The metaphor of the mountain recurs in "Contra el estío" (94) which expresses the poet's weariness with a life that has been a constant struggle to scale the heights, a struggle that has got him nowhere since fulness of age sees him as far from the peak as he was in his infancy:

> Así tras de asir yo de la cuna a la tumba,
> por cuestas y laderas del empinado monte,
> la cruz de los sudores,
> ya atrás dejar quisiera el horrísono paso
> del humano feliz que en tu ara no derrama
> sudorípara glándula.

> Para vasallo tal la buena estrella velas,
> y aun la cima del monte en vano codiciada,
> entre tus áureos rayos,

como dádiva eterna que opulenta persiste
en el crudo aquilón y los rígidos hielos
de ajenas estaciones.

The reiterative synonyms — "por cuestas y laderas" — imply that each time he surmounts one slope it is only to find himself confronted by another, so that the peak for which he vainly longs remains as inaccessible as ever. In fact the only progression he can look forward to is that which will take him from the cradle to the grave as he grows old in harness without reaching his desired goal, and the assonance running "cuna" and "tumba" into each other insinuates that the intervening years are but a mere parenthesis in which life is never fully assumed. For, far from enabling him to attain the state of well-being to which he aspires, his poorly paid labours actually hinder him, since the obligatory daily grind deprives him of the time and opportunity to pursue the activities which would fulfil him. Hence work is a burden to him, a cross which he must shoulder and which incapacitates him for the climb, and the mountain is a calvary where he suffers a martyrdom of sweat and toil. Needless to say, his martyrdom is unlike Christ's passion in that there is no redemption at the end of it. Rather, like Sisyphus, he is condemned to struggle endlessly up the mountainside with his burden and never to arrive at the summit. In contrast the "happy human" who is fortunate enough to be unburdened by work — the phrase has an ironic ring to it, hinting that the unhappy poet is hardly human, since he has been degraded to the condition of a beast of burden — is able to run fleet-footed towards the summit. The sound of the latter's footsteps above him torments the poet — the harsh adjective "horrísono" translates acoustically the unpleasant sensation they produce in his ear —, for they rub in his own failure to reach the goal the other has attained. Condemned always to lag behind in this struggle to reach the top, he cannot leave the humiliating taunt of those footsteps behind him until the death for which he wearily longs at last releases him from a life of useless toil.

In this poem a second metaphor identifies the warmth of summer with the well-being that life offers. Summer appears as a deity to obtain whose favours the poet offers the sacrifice of his work, toiling under a hot sun and shedding his sweat on summer's altar. But the god denies him its favours while bestowing them on its favourite son, the "happy human", though the latter has made no sacrifice of sweat to merit them. Emitting warmth and well-being, the sun — the star of good fortune which crowns the mountain of life — dazzles and blinds the poet as he looks upwards, veiling the peak from his view. In this way summer wields the sun's rays to defend its favours against trespassers — the verb "velar" has also the secondary sense of "to watch over" — and guard them for its favourite. And not only does it grant to the latter the divine gift of well-being but it grants it in perpetuity as a state of grace which will sustain him all his life, so that while the poet has nothing to look forward to but the chill winter of a miserable old age, the happy human will continue to luxuriate in the summer warmth till the end of his days. If the poet's struggle to climb the mountain recalls the myth of Sisyphus, the capricious behaviour of the god summer in rejecting his sacrifice while lavishing unmerited favouritism on another brings in associations with the biblical myth of Cain and Abel, thus placing the injustice of which the poet is victim within a great pattern of eternal and universal injustice.

Since the social order mirrors the fundamental injustices of life, Belli is able to establish a parallel between his own social position and the infirmity of his brother Alfonso. As Sologuren observes, "La invalidez de aquél va a extenderse analógicamente a otra condición diferente — la pobreza — coincidentes ambas en un punto común: el duro sometimiento, el avasallamiento, la servidumbre."[3] Thus, "A la zaga" (79) equates the two brothers in their common destiny:

> . . . pasando los años me he quedado
> a la zaga, ¡oh hermano!, y ya a tu par,
> codo a codo, pie a pie, seso a seso,
> hoy me avasallan todos . . .

Like Alfonso's paralysis, the poet's economic servitude is a condition which prevents him from leading a free and full life and exposes him to being bossed and pushed around by others.

In other poems the poet resembles his brother in that he quite simply has not been endowed with the qualities necessary to triumph in life. Like Alfonso he has been born deficient and though by some miracle he has managed to survive, that deficiency disqualifies him from enjoying the pleasures of the good life, which are the prize of the strong and successful:

> Una desconocida voz me dijo:
> "no folgarás con Filis, no, en el prado,
> si con hierros te sacan
> del luminoso claustro, feto mío;"
> y ahora que en este albergue arisco
> encuéntrome ya desde varios lustros,
> pregunto por qué no fui despeñado,

---

3. Javier Sologuren, *Tres poetas, tres obras. Belli — Delgado — Salazar Bondy* (Lima: Instituto Raúl Porras Barrenechea, 1969), p.14.

> desde el más alto risco,
> por tartamudo o cojo o manco o bizco.   (45)

"Sextina del mea culpa" (105) identifies this deficiency as an impractical mind:

> desde que por primera vez mi seso
> entretejió la malla de los hechos,
> con las torcidas sogas de la zaga,
> . . . cautivo yazgo hasta la muerte.
>
> De los oficios y el amor en zaga,
> por designio exclusivo de mi seso,
> me dejan así los mortales daños.

"La zaga", one of Belli's favourite expressions, brings out his failure in a competitive world, implying that the struggle for life is a rat-race in which he lags behind everyone else. This failure is attributed to the inadequacy of his intelligence to cope with the practical problems of living. The process of reasoning is described as a process of weaving facts into a net. For this task the poet's slow, clumsy brain does not have at its disposal the delicate threads which are needed, but heavy ropes which twist and become entangled, so that the only net which they weave is the one which enmeshes him in a position of social inferiority.

It is to be noted that this poem attributes no value to artistic talent, for in a competitive world that talent has no practical value. Rather, the lack of a practical bent disqualifies the poet for the struggle for life and condemns him to failure. Hence, in "Epigrama II" (98), he despairs of ever freeing himself from the misery of his poverty, symbolised by the lice which swarm over his body and which not only feed on his flesh but devour his interior being:

> ¿Cuál mano, Marcio, cuál peine
> arrojará alguna vez
> de tu cabelludo cuero
> tantas arraigadas liendres?
> Pues tus piojuelos engullen
> no el polvo de las afueras,
> ni de tu cuero la grasa,
> sino la clara primicia
> de las mil lecturas varias,
> que en ti, Marcio, de los libros
> por tus ojos hasta el buche
> del insecto pasar suele,
> confinándote a la zaga.

To the unhappy poet it seems that all the books he has read and all the culture he has acquired serve only to feed his lice, to aggravate his misery. For in a society which sets no store by such things, book-learning and artistic talent are a useless liability relegating the man of letters to the bottom of the social ladder.

While Vallejo expresses his inadequacy in face of life through the persona of the child, the persona adopted by Belli is that of the eternal loser, the poor weakling whose lot it is to be pushed around and trampled on by others stronger than he and to look on sadly and enviously as they carry off the prizes he has set his heart on. In the rat-race of life it is he who is fated always to lag in the rear:

"... postrero en todo he llegado." (93)

"... inmóvil yazgo siempre en zaga." (106)

While his more fortunate rival scales the heights of life to bask in the warm glow of success and to savour its fruits, he struggles vainly to make headway up the mountain-side, toiling and sweating under a hot summer sun for a miserable pittance; and since in this competitive world it is only those whom life favours with economic success who can hope to win women's hearts, the beautiful lady of his dreams becomes more and more inaccessible to him as he becomes more and more bogged down in his poverty:

> Entre tanto del fisco bajo el severo ceño,
> gordas gotas botando por razón de tus dardos,
> mal heme asalariado,
> o a la zaga de Filis en lustros más que nunca,
> que sólo por secuaz tuyo el feliz tal vez
> su corazón conquista. (94)

Thus the corollary of his social inferiority is rejection in love, since his poverty earns him the scorn of the women after whom he lusts:

> Ya por doquiera perseguí cual loco
> mañana, tarde, noche a bella Filis,
> mas mis hocicos su desdén cuan fiero
> restregó siempre. (103)

Brooding on his misfortunes, he comes to feel that he is the last and the lowest, the humblest and most miserable of the human species, and that the whole of humanity has ganged together to do him down:

> pienso yo muchas veces,
> que entre sí hayan pactado
> desde su edad primera,
> para prevaler sobre mí no más,
> el extraño, el amigo o el hermano. (56)

He sees himself as the "más avasallado de la tierra" (73), suffering "cual casi nadie en este crudo siglo" (104), and singled out to perform the most arduous and humiliating labours:

> . . . de abolladuras ornado estoy
> por faenas que me habéis señalado
> tan sólo a mí y a nadie más ¿por qué? (67)

One of his characteristic techniques — that of rounding off an enume-
ration with a punch-line introducing an unexpected element — em-
phasises his sense of abject inferiority. Not only do his elders, his
contemporaries and his youngers lord it over him but even those who
have still to be born into the world:

> hoy me avasallan todos y amos tengo
> mayores, coetáneos y menores,
> y hasta los nuevos fetos por llegar. (79)

So low is he on the social ladder that even his lice and their as yet
unhatched offspring are more than he: he finds himself

> . . . a la zaga,
> no sólo del piojo, no,
> mas sí de sus huevecillos. (98)

At times, indeed, Belli tends to wallow in his misery, as if he found
some kind of self-justification in suffering more than anyone else. As
Cisneros perceptively observes, "El ya se ha otorgado un lugar: ser el
peor de todos, el más débil, como una forma de individualización."[4] It
would seem that, unable to achieve self-affirmation through success, the
poet seeks it in failure and inferiority.

Employing classical language, metres and techniques, Belli intro-
duces us in his verse into a stylised rural world reminiscent of much
Spanish poetry of the Golden Age. The poet, after the manner of
Garcilaso in his "Eglogas", appears as a shepherd tending his sheep in
the valley. The characters often bear classical names such as Marcio,
Anfriso, Filis,[5] and their world is ruled by mythological deities. Happi-
ness is conceived in terms of pagan *joie de vivre* and bucolic frolicking
in the fields, but the tone of the poems tends to be elegiac. On one level
this stylised pastoral world stands as a poetic symbol of Peru seen as a
country which is still basically feudal. Reference to the mistiness of the
valley identifies it as the valley of Lima (96), and it is presented as a
cold, arid, inhospitable land where the poet-shepherd is the serf of cruel
feudal lords, "los amos". As Sologuren has observed, two recurrent
images translate this "vivencia del avasallamiento".[6] The image of "el
pie sobre el cuello" expresses the humiliating subjugation of the poet

4. Antonio Cisneros, "Por el monte abajo", *Amaru*, Lima, 1 (1967), 91.
5. Thus the poet addresses himself as Marcio (95, 98); his brother Alfonso
   appears as Anfriso (67, 79); Filis is sometimes the ideal woman of his dreams
   (45, 88) and sometimes his wife (67).
6. Sologuren, p.21.

who abases himself under the feet of his masters:

> con el chasis yo vivo de mi cuello
> bajo el rollizo pie del hórrido amo.　　(80)

The image of the trap conveys the bondage of a serf tied to the land where he was born into slavery and where he must toil all the days of his life:

> ... en el globo sublunar yacía,
> en los cepos cautivo
> del neblinoso valle de mi cuna.　　(96)

Here the circumlocution "globo sublunar" is reminiscent of the tendency of Garcilaso, Luis de León and other Golden-Age poets to avoid the obvious, but it also introduces the idea of the distance between the earth and the heavenly spheres. The earth to which the poet-shepherd is tied is far from the heavens and, since the valley is shrouded in mist, the heavens cannot even be seen. Thus the poem indicates that he is so completely absorbed by the daily economic struggle that higher things have no place in his life.

As a counterpoint to this feudal valley of tears Belli introduces into his poetic world an earthly paradise which he calls Bética, a name which evokes ancient Andalusia and the literary prestige of that region. Bética has all the characteristics of the *beatus ille* of classical literature: it is a veritable arcadia, a green, fertile, pleasant land where "el félice bético pastor" (65) lives in liberty and abundance and enjoys a permanent idyll of love. Bética, in short, is a compendium of all the poet's desires, a projection of his dreams of liberty and personal fulfilment. It is a poetic symbol of the ideal world he longs for, but which he can know only in his imagination since the real world in which he lives is very different. His land is a desolate "Bética no bella" (67), "un vasto campo mustio/de pan llevar ajeno" (90), where he lives "a la orilla fiera/del Betis que me helaba" (89), an icy torrent which resembles the Lethe rather than the cool, gently flowing Betis which waters the mythical arcadia (79). There he is enslaved by "crudos zagales" who deprive him of the freedom to write, dance and copulate (67), and he knows none of the pagan pleasures in which the "bético pastor" is able to indulge:

> nosotros ... no vamos
> por el valle gritando:
> ¡que viva el vino!, ¡que viva la cópula!　　(47)

Bética, therefore, may be regarded as a poetic device which serves to highlight by contrast the poet's frustration and the imperfections of the world he lives in.

Anachronism is an important element in Belli's work in that within the archaic pastoral world of his poetry are to be found the trappings of a modern urban civilisation. This anomaly, in fact, reflects the anomalies of many Latin American countries where progress and backwardness frequently exist side by side. Hence, if Peru appears in his poetry as a society which is still basically feudal, it appears also as a modern society ruled by impersonal economic laws which reduce man to a mere cog in the great socio-economic machine. Thus, the exchanges of "¡Abajo las lonjas!" (47) represent an inhuman commercial system which disregards every value that is not economic:

> ¡Oh Hada Cibernética!,
> cuándo de un soplo asolarás las lonjas,
> que cautivo me tienen,
> y me libres al fin
> para que yo entonces pueda
> dedicarme a buscar una mujer
> dulce como al azúcar,
> suave como la seda,
> y comérmela en pedacitos,
> y gritar después:
> " ¡abajo la lonja del azúcar,
> abajo la lonja de la seda!"

In the sugar and silk that are bought and sold in the exchanges the poet sees symbols of the softness and sweetness of woman, of the tenderness for which he longs. But it is a tenderness of which he is starved, for he is the slave of the work exacted from him by a system which exploits the individual as a mere unit of production and takes no account of his human needs. Hence he calls for the destruction of the exchanges and all that they stand for, and indulging in wish-fulfilment, he dreams of a liberated future in which he can satisfy his hunger for love and dance with gleeful triumph amid the ruins of the system he detests.

To symbolise modern economic forces Belli installs as the supreme deity of his poetic world an invented personage, Fisco, the god of income, to whom man offers up the sacrifice of his labours in the hope of winning the blessing of his generosity. In this way modern man's slavery to work is presented as a cult to a pagan god. Thus, the poet prostrates himself at the altar of Fisco only to see his offering received with disdain:

> Tal cual un can fiel a su dueño sólo,
> así a tus plantas por la vil pitanza
> que dan tus arcas, cuán cosido vivo,
> año tras año.

> Pues por el monto destos bofes míos,
> migas me lanzas como si no humanos
> fuéramos yo, mi dama y mis hijuelas,
> mas sólo hormigas.   (97)

These lines illustrate the interplay of classical and contemporary expressions that is so characteristic of Belli's verse. Colloquial terms such as "pitanza" and "bofes" alternate with archaic phrases like "plantas", "destos", "dama" etc. The classical elements refer us, by association, to a world of antiquity, where, in spite of the tyranny of the gods, man has a sense of forming part of a universal order, and where he is impelled by noble ideals and bears up to misfortune with dignity and courage. The colloquial expressions, however, refer us back to a reality which is very different, a world governed by the god of money where the individual's whole existence is absorbed by the struggle to earn a living. In short, we are shown a world where the noble ideals of former times have been replaced by base economic necessities and where dignified stoicism in face of adversity has given way to neurotic worries about making ends meet. Here, as in much of Belli's poetry, the classical tone serves ironically to underline the baseness and mediocrity of modern life.

Just as the mythical arcadia of Bética stands in opposition to a cruel feudal world, so Belli creates a counterpoint to Fisco in the Hada Cibernética. A personification of science which one day will free man from the routine of work, this figure plays in Belli's poetry the role of the fairy godmother of children's tales. One day she will descend to earth to redeem man and the poet impatiently awaits the arrival of this new Messiah:

> ¡Oh Hada Cibernética!, ya líbranos
> con tu eléctrico seso y casto antídoto,
> de los oficios hórridos humanos.   (62)

In a prophetic vision he evokes a future in which, liberated by the Hada Cibernética, he will fulfil himself as a human being. Symbols of this future state are his hands which no longer perform the mechanical tasks of clerking but joyfully transcribe the verses dictated by his poetic inspiration, and his body which no longer aches with frustration but basks in the soothing feeling of well-being which follows the realisation of the sexual act:

> Oh Hada Cibernética
> cuando harás que los huesos de mis manos
> se muevan alegremente
> para escribir al fin lo que yo desee
> a la hora que me venga en gana

> y los encajes de mis órganos secretos
> tengan facciones sosegadas
> en las últimas horas del día
> mientras la sangre circule como un bálsamo
> a lo largo de mi cuerpo   (32)

Rather than express a genuine faith in the redemptive power of science, the Hada Cibernética operates as a poetic device similar to Bética. On the one hand, it is an expression of the poet's longings projected forward into a mythical future; on the other, since the Hada Cibernética is another Godot who never arrives, it ceases to be a symbol of liberation and serves instead to throw into relief the frustrations of the present.

It has been observed that Belli's stylised classical manner serves at times to create a picture of a feudal society and at others to highlight by contrast the baseness of modern life. On other occasions, however, his use of classical forms is much more complex. Thus Julio Ortega points out that "transpuestas a una atmósfera opresiva y desintegradora, al tenso mundo moderno de sus poesía, esas formas . . . adquieren un valor de contradicción."[7] This is nowhere more evident than in "Cupido y Fisco" (103), a poem which reveals a tension that is peculiar to much of Belli's work:

> El sol, la luna y el terrestre globo
> recorrí cuánto arriba abajo ansioso,
> del ara en pos de los antiguos dioses
> Cupido y Fisco.
>
> Asaz temprano comenzó este caso,
> cuando bisoño era y tener quería
> un cuerpo y alma de mujer en casa,
> y un buen salario.
>
> Ya por doquiera perseguí cual loco
> mañana, tarde, noche a bella Filis,
> mas mis hocicos su desdén cuán fiero
> restregó siempre.
>
> Ya letra a letra el abecé retuve,
> que a la pirámide del torvo Fisco
> presto lleváronme, y de cuyas bases
> salir no puedo.
>
> Ahora, en fin, en la madura, ahora,
> ¡ay!, ¿por qué migas en amor y paga,
> si desde tiempo yo a Cupido y Fisco
> cosido yazgo?

The whole poem, in fact, is based on a tension between the mundane

7. Julio Ortega, "La poesía de Carlos Germán Belli", *Imagen*, Caracas, 33 (1968), 24.

and the noble, between modern and ancient, between the poet's real situation and the allegorical expression of it. This tension is reflected in the very title, which brings together Cupid, an authentic deity of classical mythology, and Fisco, an apocryphal deity invented by the poet to symbolise modern commercialism. It is reflected, too, in the language and style. Throughout the composition Belli attempts to create a classical tone by the use of archaic or archaic-sounding words like "en pos de", "asaz", "doquiera", "cual", "fiero", "torvo", "presto", "yazgo", etc. The circumlocution "terrestre globo" and the hyperbaton "del ara en pos de" remind us of Golden-Age verse. Like several other compositions in the book the poem consists of five *estrofas sáficas* and has a certain classical symmetry: the first two stanzas refer to Cupid and Fisco, the third and fourth deal with them separately, and the last brings them together again; each stanza is rounded off by a short last line. At the same time, this classical tone is offset by harsh or prosaic expressions like "este caso", "en casa", "un buen salario", "hocicos", "restregó", "abecé", "paga".

With regard to the theme, the second stanza states it baldly in prosaic terms: from his early youth the poet has longed for a woman of his own who will give him domestic happiness and for a good salary which will afford him a certain degree of comfort. The rest of the poem is an allegorical version of this theme. The opening stanza presents the poet as a man who has traversed the universe on a pilgrimage in search of the shrine of the gods of love and earnings. The enumeration of the planets in line one, reinforced in the second by the expression "cuánto arriba abajo", gives an epic dimension to his search and brings to mind the adventures of the Knights of the Round Table in their quest for the Holy Grail. The third stanza evokes the poet's mad pursuit of the ideal woman of his dreams and his disdainful rejection by her and thus introduces associations of the neo-platonic verse of Garcilaso and Herrera. In the fourth stanza the allegory takes us back to ancient Egypt where the Pharaohs employed slave labour to erect monuments to themselves, and the poet, who despite his education occupies a menial post, is presented as a slave who has painfully memorised the hieroglyphics so that he might adorn the walls of Fisco's pyramid and who lives enclosed within its interior endlessly working without hope of release or reward.

As a result of the tension which runs through the poem, the composition continually oscillates between two poles. The humble and mundane ambitions expressed in the second stanza reflect the mediocrity of modern life and the limited horizons of an individual reduced to an insignificant and impotent entity within the great socio-economic machine. Yet, from one point of view, there is a certain pathetic grandeur in the efforts of the average man to achieve his humble ambitions. Hence the poet elevates his situation to the level of an epic by transposing it to a stylised world of antiquity where his poverty and alienation are attributed to the cruelty of the gods and his struggle to realise his mediocre aspirations becomes a quest for noble ideals as heroic in its way as the adventures of the knights errant of old. At the same time, however, a sense of realism obliges the poet to recognise his situation for what it is and the allegory is repeatedly undermined by phrases which bring the poem back down to earth. Thus the second stanza reduces the epic quest of the first to commonplace longings, while in the third stanza the image of scorn being rubbed in the poet's snout exposes the beautiful lady of his dreams as a class-conscious snob and his platonic love for her as the humiliating frustration of animal lust. Belli's best poetry creates a tension between two contradictory views of the daily economic struggle, dignifying it as an epic struggle of the human spirit to triumph over adversity while simultaneously emphasising the squalid meanness of a routine which degrades the individual and prevents him from realising his humanity.

Unfortunately, Belli is often guilty of a certain lack of artistic rigour in that he tends to allow himself to be carried away by his liking for certain expressions and ideas, so that themes, images and words repeat themselves again and again in the course of his work. In *El pie sobre el cuello* the image of the trap ("cepo") occurs no less than thirteen times, while the expression "a la zaga" is repeated ten times with variants, and "mal mi grado" seven times. The image of the mortar appears in three poems in the space of two pages (56-57), and that of the hare-lip in two consecutive poems (92). "Una desconocida voz" (45) and "Poema" (70) both have the same central image, that of the foetus dashed to pieces from the top of a cliff, and the last line is identical in both cases. Yet this failing, as much as his virtues, provides us with a key for understanding his work. For Belli's poetry revolves obsessively around the same basic situations to express the alienation of a man trapped in an intolerable predicament from which he cannot break free.

4

ANTONIO CISNEROS

In "Crónica de Lima",[1] a poem reminiscent in some ways of Belli's "Cepo de Lima", Antonio Cisneros (b. 1942), though still only in his mid-twenties, judges his life to have been a failure and attributes that failure to the enervating atmosphere of his native city. With a nostalgia ill-befitting his years and which he plays down by employing a mock-heroic tone, he looks back on his childhood and adolescence as a period of adventure, dreams and illusions that have come to nothing:

Aquí están escritos mi nacimiento y matrimonio, y el
    día de la muerte
del abuelo Cisneros, del abuelo Campoy.
Aquí, escrito el nacimiento del mejor de mis hijos,
    varón y hermoso.
Todos los techos y monumentos recuerdan mis batallas
    contra el Rey de los Enanos y los perros
celebran con sus usos la memoria de mis remordimientos.
                    (Yo también
harto fui con los vinos innobles sin asomo de vergüenza
    o de pudor, maestro fui
en el Ceremonial de las Frituras.)

The tone is indicative of Cisneros' tendency to direct irony against himself as well as against society at large. For one of the most engaging features of his poetry is the honesty with which he recognises his own failings and questions his own position. Alongside the political battles of his youth — his involvement in the opposition to the administration of Manuel Prado (1956-62), the champion of the Peruvian oligarchy whose politics and diminutive stature earn him the scornful title of "King of the Dwarves" —, he recalls the less idealistic side of those years, the adolescent *machismo* that led to feats of over-indulgence in the pleasures of the flesh, lapses which are brought back to his mind by the spectacle of dogs licking their vomit in the street.

The second stanza sets the poet's thwarted ambitions in their social context and the irony becomes savage as it is directed against

---

1. Cisneros, *Canto ceremonial contra un oso hormiguero* (Havana: Casa de las Américas, 1968), p.19. Henceforth this volume will be identified by the abbreviation *CC*.

Lima, a city which in his eyes is capable of producing only mediocrities:

> Oh ciudad
> guardada por los cráneos y maneras de los reyes que
>   fueron
> los más torpes — y feos — de su tiempo.
>   Qué se perdió o ganó entre
>   estas aguas.
> Trato de recordar los nombres de los Héroes, de los
>   Grandes Traidores.
> Acuérdate, Hermelinda, acuérdate de mí.

Lima, the ancient vice-regal capital of South America, preserves the remains and traditions of its colonial past, but Cisneros will admit of no grandeur or splendour in that heritage. With the scathing judgement of a man embittered, he insists that the vice-roys were as inept as governors as they were ugly as men and that they set a pattern of mediocrity which has characterised his country's history ever since, a history in which he can recall no great names since the environment of Lima discourages the undertaking of great enterprises.

The refrain of the old *vals criollo* "Hermelinda", identified in the poet's mind with the carefree sprees of adolescence, serves as a device around which the poem is structured to convey in a novel manner the traditional theme of nostalgia for the golden days of youth. Addressing Hermelinda as an absent friend from a lost past, he describes to her their old haunts as they appear to him now through eyes from which the scales of illusion have fallen:

> Las mañanas son un poco más frías,
> pero nunca tendrás la certeza de una nueva estación
> — hace casi tres siglos se talaron los bosques y los pastos
> fueron muertos por fuego.
>   El mar está muy cerca,
>   Hermelinda,
> pero nunca tendrás la certeza de sus aguas revueltas,
>   su presencia
> habrás de conocerla en el óxido de todas las ventanas,
> en los mástiles rotos,
> en las ruedas inmóviles,
> en el aire color rojo-ladrillo.
>   Y el mar está muy cerca.
> El horizonte es blando y estirado.
>   Piensa en el mundo
> como una media esfera — media naranja, por ejemplo — sobre
>   4 elefantes,
> sobre las 4 columnas de Vulcano.
>   Y lo demás es niebla.
> Una corona blanca y peluda te protege del espacio exterior.

Taking the physical environment as reflecting the psychological atmosphere, Cisneros portrays Lima as a city characterised by its characterlessness. The phrase "nunca tendrás la certeza", used first in connection with the seasons and repeated a few lines later with reference to the sea, points to a general amorphousness in which nothing stands out with a clearly defined personality of its own. The seasons are virtually indistinguishable one from another, for, since the valley of Lima was denuded of vegetation centuries ago, there are only slight variations in temperature to indicate changes in the year. Likewise the sea is barely noticeable but for the corrosive dampness in the air, for it stretches out smooth and unruffled as far as the eye can see till the earth resembles the static semi-sphere of Hindu cosmogony. Traditionally the sea is associated with movement, energy, passion, but here it is identified with a bland inertia which saps Lima's vitality, and the mist which wraps the city in a protective blanket hangs in the sky like a great heraldic device of a way of life which is comfortable and safe but unadventurous and devoid of higher perspective. The Rimac, a river without water, is presented as another symbol of the lack of vitality which lies at the core of the city where everything remains in a state of unrealised potential and projects never come to fruition, and the Limeñans' optimistic assurances that this year's drought is exceptional and that next year the waters will flow are satirised as being symptomatic of a procrastinating mentality which talks always in terms of the future:

Hay, además, un río.
Pregunta por el Río, te dirán que ese año se ha secado.
Alaba sus aguas venideras, guárdales fe.

At the end of the stanza Cisneros makes explicit for the first time the parallel between the physical and psychological atmosphere of the city. In the damp air of which the Limeñans are always grumbling there is a corrosion much more insidious and destructive than rust, something which eats at the will, energy and initiative of the population, so that, even before they are formulated, desires and undertakings get lost in an aimless drifting:

Este aire — te dirán —
tiene la propiedad de tornar rojo y ruinoso cualquier
        objeto al más breve contacto.
Así,
tus deseos, tus empresas
                    serán una aguja oxidada
antes de que terminen de asomar los pelos, la cabeza.
Y esa mutación — acuérdate, Hermelinda — no depende

> de ninguna voluntad.
> El mar se revuelve en los canales del aire,
> el mar se revuelve,
> es el aire.
>   No lo podrás ver.

The last stanza brings us back to the poet as he recalls the days when he was courting the girl who was to be his wife and had a sense of vocation in life and the future seemed bright. The pebbles which he hurled into the sea symbolise the passionate enthusiasm of a youth who believed he was going to cause a ruffle in the general stagnation and set the world on fire, but that memory is linked in his mind with the things on which he has since dispersed his energies and with the great many more things which he never got round to doing. For all his high hopes he has made nothing of his life but has succumbed to the insidious lethargy which claims everyone in Lima as a victim:

> Mas yo estuve en los muelles de Barranco
> escogiendo piedras chatas y redondas para tirar al agua.
> Y tuve una muchacha de piernas muy delgadas. Y un
>   oficio.
> Y esta memoria — flexible como un puente de barcas —
>   que me amarra
> a las cosas que hice
> y a las infinitas cosas que no hice,
> a mi buena o mala leche, a mis olvidos.
>   Qué se ganó o perdió entre
>   estas aguas.
> Acuérdate, Hermelinda, acuérdate de mí.

Throughout the poem the allusions to the *vals* have played an ambivalent role, conveying the poet's nostalgia yet at the same time ironically playing down and deprecating that nostalgia by equating it with the maudlin sentimentality of the popular song. By the end of the poem, however, they have shed their ironic connotations and the plea of the last line expresses the unashamed anguish of a man whose youthful illusions and enthusiasm are irretrievably lost in the past.

A remark made by Cisneros on Belli's poetry points to a fundamental difference between the work of the two men: "La problemática de Belli es individual. Los males originados por el contexto familiar, social, se vuelven importantes y feroces solo en la medida que lo golpean directamente."[2] While Belli is temperamentally apolitical and is concerned first and foremost with his personal circumstances, Cisneros

2. Cisneros, "Por el monte abajo", *Amaru*, Lima, 1 (1967), 91.

consciously sets his alienation in a social and political context. *Comentarios Reales* (1964), his first major work, adopts the title of the famous sixteenth-century chronicle of the Inca Garcilaso de la Vega to present an alternative version of Peruvian history, one which ironically exposes time-honoured patriotic clichés as myths disguising a sordid reality of dishonesty, oppression and injustice. The volume shows the clearly marked influence of Bertolt Brecht, but significant, too, is that of Wáshington Delgado who, in poems like "Historia del Peru",[3] anticipated Cisneros in demystifying his nation's history. In "El Extranjero" Delgado speaks of his sense of being a foreigner in his own country since Peru has never been for him a true homeland with which he can identify with pride. He peruses its history and traditions in search of some positive value which would restore his faith in it, but in the past he can find nothing worthy of respect to offer him hope for the future:

> Pregunto por mi patria
> y mi esperanza busca una palabra, el nombre
> de una ciudad antigua, de una calle pequeña,
> de una fecha de victoria o desolación . . .

> Si toda esperanza surge del pasado
> nada en verdad poseo . . .[4]

Comentarios Reales is to be understood in the same vein. Though Cisneros does not speak directly of his own emotions in these historical pieces, history is in fact a medium for expressing his alienation from a society built on inglorious traditions and bankrupt of values to which he can adhere.

In an interview Cisneros has stated that "mi país tiene un pasado fabuloso, mas esa cultura ya no me pertenece y sólo puedo apreciarla en sus restos como cualquier extraño".[5] Against the tendency of many of his compatriots to seek their national roots in the early indigenous cultures, he is unable to identify with a past which he feels to be too remote to have any relevance to a twentieth-century city-dweller. This gulf divorcing past from present is the theme of "Paracas",[6] where the poetic emotion is conveyed through an evocation of a coastal scene in the area which was the site of one of Peru's earliest civilisations. Gulls feed on the miniscule sea-creatures borne by the incoming tide till they

3. Wáshington Delgado, *Un mundo dividido* (Lima: Casa de la Cultura del Perú, 1970), p.160.
4. Ibid., p.52.
5. Quoted in Leonidas Cevallos Mesones, *Los nuevos* (Lima: Editorial Universitaria, 1967), p.14.
6. Cisneros, *Comentarios Reales* (Lima: Ediciones de la Rama Florida y Ediciones de la Biblioteca Universitaria, 1964), p.11. Henceforth this volume will be designated by the abbreviation *CR*.

are bloated and bob about like boats on the waves. The landscape is devoid of all human presence and the only signs that there was once a civilisation here are a few rags and skulls:

> Desde temprano,
> crece el agua entre la roja espalda
> de unas conchas
>
> y gaviotas de quebradizos dedos
> mastican el muymuy de la marea
>
> hasta quedar hinchadas como botes
> tendidos junto al sol.
>
> Sólo trapos
> y cráneos de los muertos, nos anuncian
>
> que bajo estas arenas
> sembraron en manada a nuestros padres.

The poem transmits a sense of the littleness of man within the eternal scheme of the universe, of the impermanence of human achievements, of man's failure to leave any lasting mark on his world. The slightly ambiguous adverbial phrase of the first line hints that the events described have been taking place not only since early morning but from the very dawn of time, that they are part of an unending natural cycle which preceded man's arrival on the scene and continues long after his disappearance. Today the coastal desert remains as barren as it always was, unaltered by the civilisation which once flourished there and which has since been swallowed up by its sands. The ironic use of the verb "sembrar" in the last line insinuates that the Indians of Paracas have sown nothing which has taken root to be inherited by later generations and that all they have left behind them are the signs of their extinction. The placing of the emotive phrase "nuestros padres" in a climactic position at the end of the poem emphasises how difficult it is for a modern Peruvian to regard as his forefathers a people so long and so totally extinct.

If the poem intimates that it is futile to look for a meaningful national heritage in the distant past, it also presents an unromantic view of those ancient times. For the last line, which seems to attribute the extermination of the Indians of Paracas to genocidal warfare waged by an enemy tribe, inserts primitive human society within the pattern of the elemental natural world whose cruel laws, mirrored at the beginning of the poem in the voracity of the gulls, impel species to prey on species. Underlying the poem, therefore, is a scepticism with regard to utopian idealisations of the pre-Columbian civilisations fabricated out of disgust with Peru's European colonial heritage. This scepticism is much more explicit in "Trabajadores de tierras para el sol" (*CR* 13), which refutes the myth that the Inca period was a national golden age brought to an end by the arrival of the *conquistadores*. Stating that it was not piety but intimidation by autocratic rulers which motivated the Indians who toiled for the upkeep of the state religion, Cisneros implies that the tradition of exploitation by an unholy alliance of Church and State, commonly believed to have been introduced by the Spaniards, can in fact be traced back to the falsely glorified Inca past:

> Sabían
> que el sol
> no podía
> comer
> ni siquiera
> un
> retazo
> de choclo,
> pero evitaron
> el fuego,
> la estaca
> en
> sus
> costillas.

Even less than in its indigenous origins can Cisneros discover anything worthy of admiration in Peru's Spanish colonial heritage. Thus "Cuestión de tiempo" (*CR* 20) strips the Conquest of its legendary glory as a stirring epic of human endeavour and achievement:

I

> Mal negocio hiciste, Almagro.
> Pues a ninguna piedra
> de Atacama podías pedir pan,
> ni oro a sus arenas.
> Y el sol con sus abrelatas,
> destapó a tus soldados
> bajo el hambre
> de una nube de buitres.

II

> En 1964
> donde tus ojos barbudos
> sólo vieron rojas tunas,
> cosechan — otros buitres —
> unos bosques
> tan altos de metales,
> que cien armadas de España
> por cargarlos
> hubieran naufragado bajo el sol.

The poem presents Almagro, joint leader with Pizarro of the Spanish expedition to Peru, as the victim of a joke played by destiny. Assigned the southern half of the Inca Empire in a division of territories, he was confronted by barren desert when he went to explore his domains, and to cap the irony, others who followed in his footsteps centuries later were to discover wealthy mineral deposits where he and his men encountered only hunger and hardship. Against the traditional picture of the *conquistadores* as epic giants who came, saw and conquered, the deflating account of their ordeals in the first stanza — where survival displaces the greed for gold as their main priority and an anachronistic metaphor likens them, as they swelter in their armour under a merciless sun, to tins of sardines heated and opened to feed the vultures — and the historical perspective of the second ironically reduce them to puny creatures defeated by the continent they came to dominate and made mock of by time when they thought to immortalise themselves by their deeds. No less than the Indians of Paracas, the *conquistadores* appear here as men who flitted briefly across the stage of history without leaving any lasting achievement behind them to mark their passing.

The poem also demolishes the myth that the Spaniards brought the benefits of Christian civilisation to the benighted savages of America. The opening line categorises the *conquistadores* as adventurers on the make come to plunder the Inca Empire of its fabulous wealth, and the juxtaposition of sixteenth and twentieth centuries implies that the one sense in which they shaped history was by handing on a legacy of rapine which has characterised the so-called advanced nations' dealings with underdeveloped America and which has persisted into modern times when international capital exploits the continent's wealth on a scale of which the Spaniards never dreamed. Yet there is an ironic hint that even in this respect their influence on history is more apparent than real. For the metaphor of the vultures which equates twentieth-century imperialism with the predators of nature suggests that rather than alter the course of history the *conquistadores* merely continued and transmitted a prehistoric heritage of elemental aggressiveness which modern man has no more learned to set aside than the primitive society referred to in "Paracas".

The Christianity which the Spaniards brought to Peru and which gave colonial society its moral justification is satirised in a series of poems entitled "Oraciones de un señor arrepentido". An accompanying note places the poems in their historical context and draws attention to the hypocrisy underlying the religiosity of the colonial ruling caste:

Durante el virreynato, cuando los grandes señores llegaban a la vejez, hartos de fechorías — o imposibilitados para ellas por sus huesos — dedicábanse a escribir poesía religiosa. Muchos trasnocharon acomodando versos, hasta coger enfermedades terribles. Así, la muerte los sorprendía en plena charla con Dios.

(*CR* 27)

"Cuando el diablo me rondaba anunciando tus rigores" (*CR* 28), one of the series, expresses the terrors of an old man haunted by visions of the Devil:

> Señor, oxida mis tenedores
> y medallas, pica estas muelas,
> enloquece a mi peluquero,
> los sirvientes
> en su cama de palo sean muertos,
> pero líbrame del diablo. Con su olor
> a cañazo y los pelos embarrados,
> se acerca hasta mi casa.
> Lo he sorprendido
> tumbado entre macetas de geranio,
> desnudo y arrugado.
> Estoy un poco gordo, Señor,
> espero tus rigores, mas no tantos.
> He envejecido en batallas,
> los ídolos han muerto.
> Ahora, espanta al diablo,
> lava estos geranios y mi corazón,
> hágase la paz, amén.

Though his fear of damnation is genuine, the aged *gran señor* is incapable of true repentance because he remains to the end a *gran señor* prevented by his conditioning from questioning the values of his class. Hence he speaks of his part in the oppression of the Indians as a redeeming virtue (ll.14-15) and sees nothing incongruous in having his menials suffer to atone for his sins (ll.3-5). It is not, therefore, for his crimes against humanity that he fears punishment, but for the sins of the flesh which in old age have reduced him to a debauched wreck threatened with damnation by a Devil who appears to him in his own image (ll.6-11). Moreover, the ritual humility of his prayer cannot disguise the arrogance of a man who subconsciously regards God as one of his own kind, as a great feudal lord whose relationship to him is one of mutual dues and obligations and with whom he can settle accounts as he would with any other of his class. He bargains for forgiveness of his faults, offering to make reparation in the form of physical pain or the sacrifice of his goods and chattels, among which he includes his servants. While recognising his guilt and God's right to exact punishment, he will admit only to the minor sin of gluttony (l.12) and challenges the severity of the retribution, and to justify his claim for leniency, cites a life-time in God's service subduing the natives and stamping out idolatry. The final plea, introduced by an emphatic "Ahora", is uttered with the conviction that, having done his duty by God in such major matters, he is entitled to expect God to repay the debt by overlooking his minor misdemeanours. By thus allowing the *señor* himself to betray the hypocrisy and contradictions of his faith, the poem implies that, rather than act as a moderating and civilising influence on colonial society, religion provided the vice-regal oligarchy with a moral justification for their oppression of the natives and a convenient instrument for squaring their consciences.

Independence is likewise dismissed by Cisneros as yet another false myth propagated by a creole oligarchy which exploited the sacrifice of the common people to further its own class interests. Thus, after quoting a passage from a school history book which glorifies the victory of Ayacucho as representing the liberation of America from despotism, "Tres testimonios de Ayacucho" (*CR* 57-62) shows us the event through the eyes of the ordinary men and women who bore the brunt of the war against the Spaniards. First, an unglamorous view of the battle itself is given by a soldier who recalls the carnage of his comrades, and then its tragic consequences are revealed by a mother as she wrestles to digest the confusing news that victory has given Peru to the Peruvians and that the death of her sons has left her destitute. Unfortunately, Cisneros lacks the common touch necessary to render such poems convincing and it would be difficult to disagree with William Rowe when he argues that "Los poemas que . . . expresan la conciencia popular, carecen de genuidad".[7]

Much more effective is "Tupac Amaru relegado" (*CR* 56) where he deploys his talent for irony to satirise the sham by which the generals of the patriot armies usurped the glory of the struggle for independence as their class usurped the fruits. Symbol of that sham are the heroic whiskers sported by the so-called liberators who gave themselves martial airs as they played at soldiers at a safe distance from the battlefields and whose actual experience of war was limited to the sight of the casualties among the lower ranks on whose blood and tears they built their reputations. Later those self-same whiskers were to dominate the image of them that was presented to posterity, growing heroically

7. William Rowe, "*Canto ceremonial*: Poesía e historia en la obra de Antonio Cisneros", *Amaru*, 8 (1968), 32.

in their portraits in proportion as the history books consecrated the sham by blowing them up intó fathers of the nation:

> Hay libertadores
> de grandes patillas sobre el rostro,
> que vieron regresar muertos y heridos
> después de los combates. Pronto su nombre
> fue histórico, y las patillas
> creciendo entre sus viejos uniformes
> los anunciaban como padres de la patria.
>
> Otros sin tanta fortuna, han ocupado
> dos páginas de texto
> con los cuatro caballos y su muerte.

In the second stanza the tongue-in-cheek tone gives way to one of laconic outrage, all the more moving for its restraint. Here the poet simultaneously deflates the reputations of the official heroes and high-lights the injustice of history by contrasting their deeds and fortunes with those of Tupac Amaru, who in 1780 led an abortive insurrection against the Spaniards which ended when he was executed by being pulled apart by four horses in Cuzco. Unlike the generals who led from behind, Tupac Amaru made the ultimate sacrifice, yet he was to merit no more than a couple of pages in the history books and these were to focus attention on his defeat and spectacular death, playing down the implications of his rebellion which aimed at achieving a measure of social justice for the Indian.[8] Thus in the particular distortion involved in the relegation of Tupac Amaru to the rank of a minor historical figure, the poem shows epitomised the process by which historians of the ruling élite have manipulated their country's past to promote and defend the interests of their class.

"Descripción de monumento, plaza y alegorías en bronce" (*CR* 82) likewise debunks the myth surrounding Independence, this time through an ironic description of one of the capital's monuments which embodies in plastic form the falsehoods propagated in the history books:

> El caballo, un libertador
> de verde bronce y blanco
> por los pájaros.
> Tres gordas muchachas:
> Patria, Libertad
> y un poco recostada
> la Justicia. Junto al rabo
> de caballo: Soberanía,

---

8. It is to be noted that recent years have seen an inversion of this tendency with the glorification of Tupac Amaru as a precursor of Independence.

Fraternidad, Buenas Costumbres
(gran barriga y laureles
abiertos en sus manos).
Modestia y Caridad
refriegan ramas
sobre el libertador,
envuelto en la bandera
verde y blanca.
Arcángeles con cuernos
de abundancia. Una placa
con el nombre del muerto,
alcalde de turno,
firmas auspiciadoras,
las batallas, presidente
y obispos. Empalados
senderos, escaleras
para uso de mendigos, oxidadas
casi a diario por los perros.
Bancas de palo, geranios, otras muchachas
(su pelo blanco y verde): Esperanza,
Belleza, Castidad,
al fondo Primavera, ficus agusanados,
Democracia. Casi a diario
también, guardias de asalto:
negros garrotes, cascos verdes
o blancos por los pájaros.

The statue of the liberator is flanked by symbolic figures representing the ideals of the Republic he brought into being, but the hollowness of those ideals is immediately hinted at by the ludicrous affectation which, in an artistic transposition of the grandiloquent rhetoric of official language, casts the symbolic maidens as great fat Amazons in mock-classical style. Certain peculiarities in the monument's construction — Justice is in a slightly recumbent position, as though bending over backwards in an attempt to make itself flexible; Democracy is relegated to a place in the background where it is virtually hidden from view — are sarcastically pointed out by the poet as Freudian slips betraying the ruling élite's predisposition hypocritically to manipulate the values it professes to revere. The shoddiness into which the monument has fallen over the years — the statue is coated with verdigris and streaked with birds' droppings, the railings rusted by the urination of dogs, the trees worm-eaten — draws an ironic contrast between the professed ideals of the independent Republic and the squalid reality of life under it, and the beggars who squat on the steps close to a plaque commemorating the sponsoring dignatories are an indictment of the social injustice at the heart of the system. The demolition of the pretence represented by the monument is completed by the final punch-lines which echo the opening lines and tie the poem neatly together. For the green-bronze liberator in the middle of the square looks down regularly on green-helmeted, truncheon-wielding riot-police who personify the ultimately repressive nature of the so-called democracy which he fathered. The excrement with which the birds bombard both his statue and the helmets of the police is an expression of the poet's contempt for and of nature's revulsion against a dishonest society which disguises injustice and oppression behind a mask of noble ideals.

By bringing us down to modern times this poem provides a useful link between the historical pieces of *Comentarios Reales* and *Canto ceremonial contra un oso hormiguero* (1968), many of whose poems refer to the contemporary political scene. The vices of the traditional ruling oligarchy are embodied in the aging homosexual of the title poem (*CC* 15-17). Little is to be gained by attempting to establish the identity of the target of the poet's satire. Much more important is the implicit parallel between the private and public lives of the oligarchy, the immorality of the one reflecting the corruption of the other. A similar figure appears in Oswaldo Reynoso's novel *En octubre no hay milagros*, in the person of Don Manuel, the country's leading financier, who shares his time between preying sexually on the youth of the poorer districts of Lima and manipulating the economic and political life of the nation,[9] and though Cisneros does not spell out the parallel between the two spheres of activity, it is clearly implied. Drawing on a long national tradition of political diatribe, he portrays the incorrigible old degenerate as an insatiable ant-eater who preys on the unwary male population of Lima:

> y ya aprestas las doce legiones de tu lengua
> > granero de ortigas
> > manada de alacranes
> > bosque de ratas veloces
> > > rojas
> > > peludas
>
> el gran mar de las babas
> oh tu lengua
> cómo ondea por toda la ciudad
> torre de babel que se desploma
> > sobre el primer incauto
> > sobre el segundo
> > sobre el tercero.

9. Oswaldo Reynoso, *En octubre no hay milagros* (Lima: Ediciones Waman Puma, 1966).

Written after the reformist Fernando Belaúnde Terry came to power in 1963, the poem depicts this personification of capitalist corruption and exploitation as an ante-diluvian monster who has somehow outlived the historical upheaval that logically should have made him extinct. For in spite of everything he can still be seen prowling around the city and his voracious tongue continues to grow:

> aún te veo en la Plaza San Martín . . .
> oh tu lengua en reposo
>   y aún se reproduce
>   despacio
>   muy despacio
>   y todavía engorda.

Denouncing the manner in which the oligarchic monster still haunts the Peruvian scene despite the loss of its political protectors, the poem takes on the form of a ritual incantation intended to scare away the beast for ever:

> Y ahora
>   no más tu madre
>   no más tu abuela
>   no más tu arcángel de la guardia
> y ahora
>   océano de las babas
>   vieja abadesa
> escucha
> escucha mi canto
> escucha mi tambor
>   no dances más.

Much of the bitterness of "Crónica de Lima" is explained by "In memoriam" (*CC* 35-37), a poem on the failure of *Acción Popular* to live up to the expectations it created. More or less at the same period as Castro was overthrowing Batista in Cuba and sending a wave of revolutionary optimism through the whole Latin-American continent, Belaúnde erupted with great dynamism on the Peruvian scene to spearhead the opposition to the oligarchic regime of Prado and to offer an alternative to APRA, gaining power in the elections of 1963 with 39% of the vote. Setting himself up as the architect of a new Peru, Belaúnde aroused great enthusiasm among the middle classes and among many young people who mistakenly believed that he would follow in Castro's footsteps and preside over Revolution in Peru. Thus, in the opening lines of the poem, Cisneros describes Belaúnde and his party as the tutelar deities of his generation and evokes the climate of optimism and euphoria of that period:

Yo vi a los manes de mi generación, a los lares, cantar
en ceremonias, alegrarse
cuando Cuba y Fidel y aquel año 60 eran apenas
un animal inferior, invertebrado.
Y yo los vi después
cuando Cuba y Fidel y todas esas cosas fueron peso y
color
y la fuerza y la belleza necesarias a un mamífero joven.
Yo corría con ellos
y yo los vi correr.

The verb "correr" not only conveys the sheer exhilaration of those
days, but, with its connotations of "rushing towards a goal" and
"running with the herd", suggests a sense of participating in a national
and continental mass movement which promised to build a brave new
world. But the poet and others like him were soon to be disabused of
the ingenuous illusion that Peru and Cuba were advancing along parallel
courses. For even as they were parading their righteous indignation
against the blockade by which the United States sought to contain the
Cuban Revolution, they were to be shocked by the death of Javier
Heraud, which demonstrated the determination of Belaúnde's reformist
government not to allow a Cuban-style revolution to develop in Peru:[10]

Y el animal fue cercado con aceite, con estacas de
pino, para que ninguno conociera
su brillante pelaje, su tambor.
Yo estuve con mi alegre ignorancia, mi rabia, mis
plumas de colores
en las antiguas fiestas de la hoguera,
Cuba sí, yanquis no.
Y fue entonces que tuvimos nuestro muerto.

Characteristically, Cisneros plays down his disillusionment at the
beginning of the second stanza by adopting a tone of cynical worldly
wisdom to suggest that it is the fate of every generation to be let down
by the idols in which it places its faith:

Quién no tuvo un par de manes, tres lares y algún
brujo como toda heredad
— sabios y amables son, engordan cada día.
Hombres del país donde la única Torre es el comercio
de harina de pescado,
gastados como un odre de vino entre borrachos.
Qué aire ya nos queda.

10. The young poet Javier Heraud (1942-1963) was a member of a detachment
of Cuban-trained guerrillas of the MIR (Movimiento Izquierdista Revolucio-
nario) who in 1963 entered Peru from Bolivia near Puerto Maldonado, with
the object of organising guerrilla activity. They were intercepted and dis-
persed by the army and Heraud was killed in the action.

Y recibimos un laurel viejo de las manos del propio
Virgilio y de manos de Erasmo
una medalla rota.
Holgados y seguros en el vericueto de la Academia y
las publicaciones.
Temiendo algún ataque del Rey de los Enanos, tensos
al vuelo de una mosca:
Odiseos maltrechos que se hicieron al agua
aun cuando los temporales destruían el sol y las manadas
de cangrejos, y he aquí
que embarraron con buen sebo la proa
hasta llegar a las tierras del Hombre de Provecho.
(Amontonad los muertos en el baño, ocultadlos, y
pronto el Coliseo
será limpio y propicio como una cama blanda.)

The noun "brujo", echoing an earlier reference to the poet's "plumas de colores", equates the charismatic Belaúnde with the witchdoctors who dupe ignorant savages with their putative magical powers. This implicit recognition that the poet and his contemporaries were the gullible victims of their own naive idealism gives way to a progressively more ironic tone as judgement is passed on the men of *Acción Popular* who betrayed the hopes of a whole generation. They are characterised as charming, intelligent, well-meaning middle-class figures whose idea of revolution boiled down in practice to reforming the existing structure to create a modern, liberal neo-capitalist state. The only religion of their "new Peru" is economic progress, exemplified by the fish-meal industry,[11] and the idealism which seemed to motivate them has exhausted itself as the middle classes wax prosperous on the crest of an economic boom. The simile of drunks clustered around an empty wine barrel graphically expresses the failure of *Acción Popular* to satisfy the country's thirst for a radical ideology, while the ironic allusion to the pestilence of the fish-meal factories conveys the contamination of the pure air of idealism by the new materialism. Irony is again present in the image of Virgil and Erasmus handing out awards, which mocks the complacency that has defrauded the expectations of a people crying out for social change by offering them instead a traditional bourgeois liberal democracy. With heavy sarcasm Cisneros describes the history of *Acción Popular* as a series of Odysseys in which each followed his individual road to success in a neo-capitalist society. For having broken through the barriers of oligarchic privilege to establish themselves and their kind in positions of wealth and influence, they have lost their

11. In the fifties and sixties Peru developed into the world's largest fishing and fishmeal-producing nation.

reforming zeal in their concern to defend the middle-class paradise they have created for themselves. Mockery is directed against their obsessive fear of an oligarchic counter-offensive led by Prado, "King of the Dwarves", and the final biting comment denounces the self-satisfied complacency with which they turn a blind eye to the regime's repression of revolutionary activity designed to achieve the very goals to which they themselves once seemed committed.

Yet the poem ends on a brave note. For though Revolution has been successfully held in check in Peru, the poet sees ground for hope in the guerrilla war that has broken out in the South and conditions ripe for revolution in the misery that is widespread in the North:

> Hay un animal noble y hermoso cercado entre ballestas.
> En la frontera Sur la guerra ha comenzado. La peste,
> el hambre, en la frontera Norte.

In the event, however, this turned out to be wishful thinking, for the guerrilla campaign proved a failure and was eventually crushed.

In the poems just examined Cisneros' alienation has a socio-political basis. Elsewhere it is related more closely to his personal circumstances, to his sense of being stifled by the stuffy conventionality of his middle-class environment. The title of "Soy el favorito de mis cuatro abuelos" (*CC* 83) alludes ironically to the doubtful honour of being a favourite grandson obliged by the pressure of family blackmail to conduct himself like the model of bourgeois virtues his grandparents imagine and expect him to be. The poem contrasts the freedom of lazing on the beach with the stiff formality of a family gathering:

> Si estiro mi metro ochentaitantos en algún hormiguero
> y dejo que los animalitos construyan una ciudad sobre
>   mi barriga
> puedo permanecer varias horas en ese estado y corretear
> por el centro de los túneles y ser un buen animalito,
> lo mismo ocurre si me entierro en la pepa de algún
>   melocotón
> habitado por rápidas lombrices. Pero he de sentarme
>   a la mesa
> y comer cuando el sol esté encima de todo: hablarán
>   conmigo
> mis 4 abuelos y sus 45 descendientes y mi mujer, y yo
>   debo
> olvidar que soy un buen animalito antes y después de
>   las comidas
> y siempre.

Luxuriating in a state of bodily well-being, the poet is so in tune with the creatures of the animal kingdom who unthinkingly follow their natural instincts that he actually feels himself to be an ant or a worm. But he must tear himself away to endure the ritual of a family lunch in a climate where formality is ridiculously out of place and, moulding his personality to the demands of the occasion, he must force himself to be sociable and to behave with proper decorum. The penultimate line is charged with irony, suggesting that although even the middle classes betray their basic animality in the act of eating, their prescription for life — to be applied before and after meals! — is to suppress one's animal nature. The final line, however, ends the poem on a sombre, defeatist note. For Cisneros the most soul-destroying feature of life in the bourgeois circles in which he has grown up is that he cannot act naturally and be himself but must play out the roles scripted for him by social convention.

The adventure of an early marriage was to lead Cisneros into a pitfall as restrictive and frustrating in its way as the family from which he sought to break away, and "La última costumbre del día"[12] describes a married life that has degenerated into empty domestic routine:

> La última costumbre del día ha terminado más rápido
>   que otras veces:
> huevo frito — con la yema blanda — arroz y un vaso de
>   leche.
> Y ahora
> cómo distraer a la manada que vive en mi pellejo,
>   qué ofrecerles
> al deseo, a la ignorancia, al remordimiento, a la cobardía,
>   a la mala voluntad
> para que dejen de chillar y hablarme de tú ante los ojos
> de Diego y mi mujer, como si fuesen viejos camaradas.
> Sólo me queda llevarlos a mi cama,
>   y yo entonces
> amarrado al potro o entre la doncella de hierro o el pantano
> he de contestar una y otra vez lo que ellos me preguntan y
>   ya saben.
> Y en mi cáscara roja pataleo como el pez-raya sobre una gran
>   pradera. Hasta quedar dormido/apachurrado/muerto.

The poem situates us at a critical moment in the poet's day. Supper — always the same insipid meal invariably cooked in exactly the same manner and quickly devoured since the spouses have lost the ability to converse with each other — constitutes yet another unchanging ritual culminating a day regulated by habit. But the daily routine at least has

12. Cisneros, *Agua que no has de beber* (Barcelona: Carlos Milla Batres Ediciones, 1971), p.75. A note to the edition describes these poems as having been written too late to include in *Comentarios Reales* and too early for inclusion in *Canto ceremonial*.

the merit of enabling the couple to keep up a pretence and to disguise from themselves the emptiness of their relationship, and the moment of truth arrives at the end of the day when they are thrown back upon themselves to spend the evening together in family intimacy. Hence the poet views the end of supper with apprehension, for, without the routine to shelter behind, he must now wrestle with the dissatisfaction that wells up inside him. All its concomitants — restlessness, aimlessness, regret at having got himself into marriage, remorse at causing pain by his discontent, a cowardly fear of doing anything drastic to free himself, surly ill-temper — nag at him like lice and, unable to placate or find distraction from them, he has no alternative but to take them to bed with him, there to submit night after night to the torture of a vicious circle of self-interrogation. The simile of the stranded ray-fish wriggling and writhing on dry land graphically conveys the predicament of the poet who feels out of his element in his marriage and restlessly tosses and turns in his bed till eventually he falls asleep from sheer exhaustion. The ambivalent last line falls like a sentence of death, implying that in the alien atmosphere of marriage the poet must either be slowly destroyed by his mental and emotional torment or undergo spiritual death by sacrificing his inner being.

Some of Cisneros' best poems are built around a central animal image. Thus, "La araña cuelga demasiado lejos de la tierra" (*CC* 89) draws a parallel between his situation and that of the spider whose universe is limited to the immediate surroundings of its web. Just as the spider dangles above the ground or scuttles about from side to side without getting very far, so the poet lives alienated in a little private world which he shares with his mate and a few friends:

> La araña cuelga demasiado lejos de la tierra,
> tiene ocho patas peludas y rápidas como las mías
> y tiene mal humor y puede ser grosera como yo
> y tiene un sexo y una hembra — o macho, es difícil
> saberlo en las arañas — y dos o tres amigos,
> desde hace algunos años
> almuerza todo lo que se enreda en su tela
> y su apetito es casi como el mío, aunque yo pelo
> los animales antes de morderlos y soy desordenado,
> la araña cuelga demasiado lejos de la tierra
> y ha de morir en su redonda casa de saliva,
> y yo cuelgo demasiado lejos de la tierra
> pero eso me preocupa: quisiera caminar alegremente
> unos cuantos kilómetros sobre los gordos pastos
> antes de que me entierren,
> y ésa será mi habilidad.

The difference between man and insect, of course, is that he is conscious of being trapped and aspires to the freedom and fulfilment associated with the wide open spaces and green grass of the earth above which the spider hovers but never reaches. Should he ever manage to attain it, he would regard it as the supreme achievement of his life.

In a manner reminiscent of Vallejo's habit of ironically deprecating his own animality, Cisneros here resists the temptation to present his alienation in a heroic light and instead offers an unflattering portrait of himself as a man bound by the weaknesses of his human nature. Here is no spiritual being thwarted in his aspirations by an intractable material world, but an ill-tempered creature whose activities, no less restricted than his field of action, revolve around the satisfaction of his sexual and alimentary appetites. If anything, the insect comes off better from the comparison, for though the voracious spider devours everything that strays into its web, even its greed cannot match the gluttony of the human, and while the man has a certain refinement and skins his food before eating it, he is also slovenly and fouls his nest in a way that the insect does not. Yet the paradox of the poem is that, despite the fact that he is unable to shake off the bonds of his bestiality, the poet is equally unable to live a free and spontaneous existence in harmony with the natural world, because he is caught in an inhibiting web by the conventions of bourgeois society and his human propensity to reason. Hence the poem ironically inverts the conventional imagery of human aspirations, which pictures man as earth-bound and longing for the heavens, to show the poet dangling in the air above an inaccessible earth. Here man is enmeshed in a web of his own making, trapped in his own fabricated world of abstract thought, unable to come down to earth and simply immerse himself in life. In a poem charged with irony the supreme irony is that man, as a civilised animal, gets the worst of both worlds.

Another allegory of the poet's circumstances is to be found in "Poema sobre Jonás y los desalienados" (*CC* 69), an imaginary account of life in the belly of a whale:

Si los hombres viven en la barriga de una ballena
sólo pueden sentir frío y hablar
de las manadas periódicas de peces y de murallas
oscuras como una boca abierta y de manadas
periódicas de peces y de murallas
oscuras como una boca abierta y sentir mucho frío.
Pero si los hombres no quieren hablar siempre de lo mismo
tratarán de construir un periscopio para saber
cómo se desordenan las islas y el mar

Poetry of Alienation: Antonio Cisneros

y las demás ballenas – si es que existe todo eso.
Y el aparato ha de fabricarse con las cosas
que tenemos a la mano y entonces se producen
las molestias, por ejemplo
si a nuestra casa le arrancamos una costilla
perderemos para siempre su amistad
y si el hígado o las barbas es capaz de matarnos.
Y estoy por creer que vivo en la barriga de alguna ballena
con mi mujer y Diego y todos mis abuelos.

The whale is a metaphor of a monstrous social order in which individuals are swallowed up by the system and held trapped in a state of physical and spiritual privation. The repetition of lines 2-6 conveys a sense of the vicious circle that is life in such a claustrophobic atmosphere: physical existence is an endless round of putting up with hardship and intellectual activity revolves around local events, alternating between grumbling against the restrictive system and excitement at periodic economic booms. The central part of the poem deals with the fate of those who cannot content themselves with such a narrow, parochial existence, who have a restless longing to broaden their horizons and discover what life is like in the outside world. To build themselves a periscope they must strip their materials from the whale's insides and in so doing they run the risk of antagonising it. The periscope is, of course, a symbol of intellectual freedom, and the implication is that thinking for oneself, having preoccupations and ideas different from those imposed by the milieu, smacks of subversion and is likely to draw down on one's head the wrath of the society which feels itself threatened. This is what Cisneros feels his own predicament to be. The title draws a distinction between the alienated poet who recognises that he is in the position of Jonah and the unthinking majority who remain blissfully unaware of their condition. The poem, therefore, is directed not only against the restrictive social system as such but also against the complacency and provincialism of the poet's fellow countrymen.

It is characteristic of Cisneros that, having adopted this heroic stance of lonely defiance, he then wrote a postscript, "Apéndice del poema sobre Jonás y los desalienados" (*CC* 73), in which he reassesses his position and debunks it as mere empty posturing. Here he recognises that, for all his brave words, he, too, in practice has followed the line of conformity and played his part in bolstering up the society which he hates. The poem shows him servilely labouring to feed the whale which shelters him and helping it to grow fat:

85

Y hallándome en días tan difíciles decidí alimentar
a la ballena que entonces me albergaba:
tuve jornadas que excedían en mucho a las
　　12 horas
y mis sueños fueron oficios rigurosos, mi fatiga
engordaba como el vientre de la ballena:
qué trabajo dar caza a los animales más robustos,
desplumarlos de todas sus escamas y una vez
　　abiertos
arrancarles la hiel y el espinazo,
　　　　　y mi casa engordaba.

(Fue la última vez que estuve duro: insulté a la
　　ballena,
recogí mis escasas pertenencias para buscar
alguna habitación en otras aguas, y ya me
　　aprestaba
a construir un periscopio,
cuando en el techo vi hincharse como 2 soles sus
　　pulmones
— iguales a los nuestros
pero estirados sobre el horizonte —, sus omóplatos
remaban contra todos los vientos,
　　　　　y yo solo,
con mi camisa azul marino en una gran pradera
donde podían abalearme desde cualquier ventana,
yo el conejo, los perros veloces atrás, y ningún
　　agujero.)
Y hallándome en días tan difíciles
me acomodé entre las zonas más blandas y
apestosas de la ballena.

The second stanza explains what lies behind his conformity. His re-
belliousness, he confesses, petered out in a whimper when, at the
moment of truth, he was made aware of his frailty in contrast to the
might of the whale. His fearful vision of being exposed and defenceless
like a hunted rabbit in the middle of a field was a warning to him of the
fate that lies in store for the individual who opts to defy society and live
outside its pale. Unable to live without the economic and psychological
security that society provides, he took cold feet and the final image of
him settling down in the whale's softest and most pestilent regions
graphically expresses the moral accommodation by which he took the
easy way out and compromised his ideals for the sake of his own peace
and comfort. The "Apéndice", therefore, reveals Cisneros to be the
victim as much of his own moral cowardice as of the social system of
which he complained in the previous poem.

　　　Eventually, however, Cisneros was to make the break which he had often contemplated. Separating from his wife and exiling himself from Peru, he lived for several years in Europe, where he taught at the universities of Southampton and Nice. His European experience provides the subject matter for many of the poems of *Canto ceremonial contra un oso hormiguero* and the later volume, *Como higuera en un campo de golf* (1972). As the latter title indicates, he was never to feel at home in Europe, being very conscious of his condition as an exotic specimen transplanted in alien soil, as a man of the Third World in a highly developed industrial culture. This is nowhere more evident than in the four short poems grouped under the title "Crónica de viaje/ Crónica de viejo".[13] While he admired the achievements of European civilisation and could not help but be impressed by the grandeur of London and Paris, he was very much aware that that culture had been built on the domination and exploitation of the underdeveloped world and that what he was in fact admiring were

> Arcos de triunfo que celebran mi condición de esclavo,
> de hijo de los hombres comedores de arroz.

Moreover, in Europe he experienced the loneliness and homesickness of the traveller who is always on the move and belongs nowhere. Hence the last poem of the series looks forward to his return to Lima at the end of his European Odyssey:

> Y yo tengo también una ciudad
> Aunque no habite nadie
> que teja y que desteja para mí
> en estas estaciones de océanos y gigantes.
> Ya el concurso
> para templar el arco se ha cerrado.
> Telémaco no habrá de conocerme
> bajo el duro pellejo del pastor.
> Mas yo he de conocerlo. Y en las calles
> alto, caminaré como si hubiese
> vencido en el combate a la serpiente,
> al puma, a la gorgona,
> al soldado más fuerte de ese reino
> del gran oso hormiguero.

He is fully aware that, unlike Ulysses, he does not have a wife patiently waiting to welcome him home and will be a stranger to the son he abandoned as a child. Nor can he boast of any exploits to match those of the Greek hero. Nor is he under any illusion that Lima will have changed in his absence but acknowledges that it is still "the kingdom

13. Cisneros, *Como higuera en un campo de golf* (Lima: Instituto Nacional de Cultura, 1972), pp.133-136.

of the great ant-eater", a society where the old pattern of exploitation still persists. Nonetheless, he will walk tall through the streets of his native city with the same pride and satisfaction that Ulysses felt on his return to his beloved Ithaca. This poem, therefore, would seem to mark a realisation on Cisneros' part that, no matter how oppressive he found Lima in the past, that is where his emotional roots are, and that he cannot flee his alienation but must come to terms with it on his home ground.[14]

14. Subsequently Cisneros was to resume his travels and to turn to Catholicism. See *El Libro de Dios y de los húngaros* (Lima: Libre-1, 1978).

PART TWO
VISIONARY POETRY

JOSE MARIA EGUREN

The first part of the book has studied the alienation of the artist in contemporary society. This second part deals with another major literary current of our times: a visionary or neo-mystical poetics[1] in which poetry is conceived as an alternative life style devoted to the passionate pursuit of self-fulfilment. For the poet-visionary poetry is an activity akin to that of the mystic: he turns his back on the world and withdraws into solitary contemplation; he devotes himself to the task of exploring the unknown, those areas of reality which lie beyond our day-to-day experience; he strives to transcend the limitations of the everyday world and to make contact with a great reality; his poetry seeks to capture the privileged moment which Pater calls "beatific vision" and Joyce "epiphany", the moment when he is fulfilled by an ecstatic sense of participating in a cosmic harmony. This poetic tradition may be regarded as an expression of the spiritual hunger of modern man alienated in a world desacramentalised by a rationally orientated civilisation. With the decline of traditional religion as an outlet for man's spiritual longings, poetry has become elevated to the category of a medium for exploring the unknown and apprehending a greater reality.

Originating with the Romantics, this concept of poetry was virtually to become a religion among the French Symbolists, whose poetics owed much to Neo-platonic theories as popularised by Swedenborg. The poet was elevated to the rank of a priest endowed with the power to see behind and beyond the objects of the material world to the essences concealed in the ideal world, and the purpose of poetry was to capture and convey by means of symbols his perceptions of the ideal world.[2] "It is through and by means of poetry," said Baudelaire,[3]

1. The term "a new mysticism" has, in fact, been used to describe this poetics in France. See Anna Elizabeth Balakian, *Literary origins of surrealism: a new mysticism in French poetry* (London: King's Crown Press, 1947).
2. This concept of poetry grows out of German philosophy of the eighteenth century. A parallel English poetic tradition is discussed by Frank Kermode in *Romantic Image* (London: Fontana, 1971).
3. Quoted by C. Chadwick, *Symbolism* (London: Methuen, 1971), p.3.

"that the soul perceives the splendours lying beyond the grave."

In Peru all the ingredients of the Symbolist poetics are to be found in the work of José María Eguren.[4] It has already been seen in the first part of the book that Eguren manifested his disconformity with his milieu by withdrawing from the world to devote himself to his artistic pursuits, and that his poetry makes a veiled criticism of a mechanistic civilisation which seemed to him to be spiritually bankrupt. However, it is, above all, a positive impulse which animates his work. The essay "Ideas extensivas" (308) suggests that there is a kind of cosmic law by which every living thing aspires to go beyond itself, attracted by the lure of what lies outside its field of vision or experience. Eguren himself experienced this restlessness of spirit and it is symbolised in his poetry by the falcons of "Los alcotanes" (44) and the migrant birds of "Alas" (116). In "La niña de la garza" (161) it is personified by a young girl who stands gazing dreamily into the distance:

> Junto al zócalo griego,
> la niña de la garza
> mira la distancia.
>
> Con sus ojos claros
> de mirares bellos,
> con ansia de vuelo.

Like the statue beside her, her body is rooted to the earth, but her spirit is the spirit of the heron and she longs to take flight towards the beautiful landscapes which she envisages beyond the distant horizon. In "El romance de la noche florida" (168) another young girl falls asleep, heedless of the romantic attractions of the moonlit garden outside, where the poet sings of his love for her. Like a kingfisher taking flight towards misty regions, her spirit embarks on a voyage through the uncharted seas of the shadowy world of dreams:

> Te apartas de mi noche florecida
> en tu bajel de sueño, como a funestas brumas
> tiende las alas el alción feliz.

The girl whose gaze is set on a distant horizon and she who prefers her dreams to "reality" may be seen as symbols of the poet's own soul which is unable to content itself with life as it is ordinarily lived and which hungers to go beyond the limits of the everyday world to experience what lies on the other side. Eguren turns his back on the world and withdraws into lonely contemplation, not merely because he is at

---

4. As in the first part of the book, all references are to Eguren, *Obras completas* (Lima: Mosca Azul Editores, 1974).

odds with society, but because his concern is not with the things of the world but with the greater spiritual reality which, it has been seen, he believed lay beyond the material.

His poetics is most clearly expressed in "Pedro de acero" (33) and "Peregrín cazador de figuras" (74), both of which present the poet as an isolated figure withdrawn from the world and as an explorer of the unknown. Thus the miner who toils to extract gold from the earth in the first poem is a symbol of the poet who delves beneath the surface of life to get to the heart of things, who labours to uncover the world's hidden marvels. The second poem introduces the figure of Peregrín who explores a dark, mysterious landscape and hunts the weird and fantastic creatures who inhabit it:

> En el mirador de la fantasía,
> al brillar del perfume
> tembloroso de armonía;
> en la noche que llamas consume;
> cuando duerme el ánade implume,
> los órficos insectos se abruman
> y luciérnagas fuman;
> cuando lucen los silfos galones, entorcho,
> y vuelan mariposas de corcho
> o los rubios vampiros cecean,
> o las firmes jorobas campean;
> por la noche de los matices,
> de ojos muertos y largas narices;
> en el mirador distante,
> por las llanuras;
> Peregrín cazador de figuras,
> con ojos de diamante
> mira desde las ciegas alturas.

The poem's nocturnal landscape may be taken as a symbol of the other side of life, those dark areas of reality which lie outside our rational experience and which cannot be illuminated or explained by the light of reason. It is, firstly, the natural world, or, more exactly, the spiritual universe which Eguren, in defiance of the mechanistic vision of a scientific age, believed lay concealed behind the material world, but at the same time it is also the poet's own inner world, the realm of the subconscious, fantasy, memory and dreams. In his prose Eguren defines beauty as "la harmonía del misterio" (246) and poetry as "la revelación del misterio por la verdad del sentimiento" (255): poetry is the revelation of the harmony which lies behind the mystery of things and which the poet apprehends intuitively. Like Peregrín, Eguren was an explorer of a dark, mysterious universe whose secrets he sought to capture in the shape of symbolic figures who would embody in synthesised form his perceptions of life's underlying harmony.

The moment of epiphany that is the goal of Eguren's poetics is celebrated in "La niña de la lámpara azul" (51). Here the protagonist not only symbolises the spirit of illusion as was seen earlier, but is also a manifestation of another dimension of reality:

En el pasadizo nebuloso
cual mágico sueño de Estambul,
su perfil presenta destelloso
la niña de la lámpara azul.

Agil y risueña se insinúa,
y su llama seductora brilla,
tiembla en su cabello la garúa
de la playa de la maravilla.

Con voz infantil y melodiosa
en fresco aroma de abedul,
habla de una vida milagrosa
la niña de la lámpara azul.

Con cálidos ojos de dulzura
y besos de amor matutino,
me ofrece la bella criatura
un mágico y celeste camino.

De encantación en un derroche,
hiende leda, vaporoso tul;
y me guía a través de la noche
la niña de la lámpara azul.

Like the genies of Arab tales, she is an apparition from a marvellous world where life is "miraculous" and, intoxicating the poet with her enchantments, she leads him along a "magical and heavenly path" to a realm of magical wonders beyond the bounds of the material world.

In general, however, the tone of Eguren's poetry is not one of ecstatic transportation but rather one of serene contemplation as the poet glimpses a cosmic order amid the beauties of the natural world. Eguren was particularly enamoured of the early dawn, the magical moment, rich with promise, when the world is poised on the brink of a new day, the moment of rebirth when life emerges anew from the womb of darkness, the moment when the miracle of creation is daily repeated. Poems like "La dama I" (23), "Los ángeles tranquilos" (52) and "Nuestra Señora de los Preludios" (198) capture the spirit of that moment through symbolic figures who imply a spiritual presence behind the material universe. In "Los ángeles tranquilos" the peaceful calm of the first moment of day is announced and highlighted by the abrupt dying down of a storm that has raged in the night:

> Pasó el vendaval; ahora,
> con perlas y berilos,
> cantan la soledad aurora
> los ángeles tranquilos.

That calm is then embodied in the persons of the tranquil angels who now make their appearance, adorned with jewels evocative of the sparkling freshness of the morning dew, and singing a hymn to the peaceful solitude that is not merely an attribute of the dawn but *is* the dawn. There is, however, a seemingly ironic contrast between their joyful hymns of praise and the scene of storm-wrought devastation revealed by the first light:

> Modulan canciones santas
> en dulces bandolines;
> viendo caídas las hojosas plantas
> de campos y jardines.

In fact the irony is only apparent. Far from being dismayed by such a spectacle, they are stimulated by it to celebrate the miracle of rebirth. The tranquil angels, therefore, do not merely symbolise the calm of dawn but are heralds of the new life which dawn daily brings forth. Antonio Cisneros has observed that much of Eguren's poetry is based on temporal progressions which follow the movement of the sun through the heavens.[5] Here there is just such a progression as the sun forces its rays through the morning mist and bathes the world in dazzling light:

> Mientras sol en la neblina
> vibra sus oropeles,
> besan la muerte blanquecina
> en los Saharas crueles.
>
> Se alejan de madrugada,
> con perlas y berilos,
> y con la luz del cielo en la mirada
> los ángeles tranquilos.

Like lost travellers shrivelled up and blanched by a merciless desert sun, the tranquil angels fade away in the heat and light of the day, for the sun's pulsating warmth signifies that the day has thrived strong and vigorous and that the moment of calm that preceded its birth has passed. The whole poem is thus informed by a sense of continuity and order, of an unending cycle in which day is continually reborn out of night and life out of death. Indeed the final stanzas open the poem out

---

5. Antonio Cisneros, "El transcurrir: un mecanismo básico de Eguren", Diss. Universidad Nacional Mayor de San Marcos, 1967, p.1.

to add a metaphysical dimension to this process. The tranquil angels who lovingly embrace death and depart with the light of heaven gleaming in their eyes become a symbol of spirit for which death in this world is the prelude to rebirth on another plane of existence. The order of the natural world, the poem suggests, mirrors a supernatural order.

"Los reyes rojos" (28) presents another vision of a cosmic order behind the workings of nature. The poem evokes two falcons locked in combat. Seen against the rays of the rising sun, they resemble warrior kings hurling golden lances at each other:

> Desde la aurora
> combaten dos reyes rojos,
> con lanza de oro.

After the opening close-up they disappear from view, but their presence is felt as their violent rage hangs in the air like a storm-cloud casting a dark shadow over the woods and mountains:

> Por verde bosque
> y en los purpurinos cerros
> vibra su ceño.

In the next two stanzas they reappear, but they are seen from a distance as minute figures silhouetted against the skyline:

> Falcones reyes
> batallan en lejanías
> de oro azulinas.
>
> Por la luz cadmio,
> airadas se ven pequeñas
> sus formas negras.

Here, as in the previous poem, there is a temporal progression, for the third stanza conjures up the setting sun in a darkening sky, while the metallic light of the fourth suggests the gathering dusk which reduces the falcons to shadowy forms. In the final stanza night has fallen and the falcons, dominating the foreground once more, are still grimly fighting:

> Viene la noche
> y firmes combaten foscos
> los reyes rojos.

The poem thus builds up a sense of a struggle that is unending and world-wide in scope: it is fought over woods and mountains and as far as the eye can see; at dawn it has already begun and it goes on into the night. The two endlessly warring birds of prey, it would seem, symbolise the violence of nature, the struggle for life, the conflict of elemental forces. However, tone is a critical factor in this poem. There is nothing to suggest that this conflict is evil. Rather the presentation of the falcons as warrior kings brings in associations of epic battles and heroic deeds and confers an awesome majesty to their struggle, while the alliterations of the last two lines convey an impression that the struggle is relentless and imperious, that it obeys some superior law. In a perceptive commentary Julio Ortega observes: ". . . estamos ante una oposición y al mismo tiempo ante una armonía; los reyes rojos luchan infatigables y sentimos que su batallar es como la trama de algo invisible; por eso no se trata de una lucha inútil o absurda, sino que hay en ella una extraña necesidad, un orden superior que la determina y funda- menta; en ello está su armonía, su acuerdo fundamental en el combate."[6] Behind the elemental struggle portrayed in the poem there is a sense of order and harmony, and the violence and conflicts of the natural world are felt to fit into a wider pattern as elements in a universal order.

Such visions of harmony, however, are fleeting and short-lived. In "Gacelas hermanas" (115) the elusive nature of this harmony glimpsed briefly behind the mystery of things is highlighted by the symbol of a pair of gazelles gliding gracefully in unison through the forest:

> ¡Gacelas hermanas!
> Eran dos; en el bosque sombrío,
> las ví en la mañana.

Later in the poem the gazelles flee in panic from the huntsmen and when, in the final stanza, the poet glimpses them for the last time it is to see them lying dead:

> Y en la tarde blanca,
> las ví muertas en claro de bosque
> ¡gacelas hermanas!

The poet's final exclamation echoes his first, but it is no longer a cry of admiration but one of regret. Beauty is felt in this poem to be a fragile thing constantly under threat and doomed inevitably to die.

Time and death, therefore, are central themes in Eguren's work. Much of his poetry is dominated by sadness, by a sense that beauty and happiness soon pass and are gone forever, by nostalgia for the lost idylls of the past. One of the principal figures of his poetry, a young girl struck down by death, stands as an emblem of this aspect of his work. His poems speak of at least three different adolescent girls whose lives ended prematurely -- his niece, a victim of tuberculosis ("Noche I", 79), another girl who died of a snake-bite ("Antigua", 69) and a third called Clara who was drowned ("El Estanque", 111) -- and it would

6. Julio Ortega, *José María Eguren*, Biblioteca Hombres del Perú, vol. XXX (Lima: Editorial Universitaria, 1965), pp.102-3.

seem that these various girls fused together in the poet's memory as a symbol of beauty cut down before it had reached full bloom. Thus, in "La muerta de marfil" (93) the poet contemplates the girl's tomb and nostalgically visualises her as she was, an adolescent blossoming into womanhood and seeing the world with the illusions of her first innocent experiences of love:

Desde el túmulo frío, de verdes oquedades,
volaba el pensamiento
hacia la núbil áurea, bella de otras edades,
ceñida de contento.
Al ver obscuras flores,
libélulas moradas, junto a la losa abierta,
pensé en el jardín claro, en el jardín de amores,
de la beldad despierta.

In other poems, such as "Casa vetusta" (15) and "La capilla muerta" (135), the poet revisits the scenes of his childhood to find with regret that everything is in a state of delapidation and decay and peopled only by ghosts and memories. In a similar vein the abandoned room of "El cuarto cerrado" (98) stands as a symbol of death and decay, as a kind of monument to the ravages of time. The atmosphere of the poem is sad and oppressive. The room is presented in terms of absence of people, movement, sounds, light and warmth, as still, silent, dark, damp and chilly. It is as if, when the room was locked up for the last time, life had been shut out of it forever. In keeping with his characteristic technique of humanising inanimate objects, Eguren personifies the room. In the absence of the people who once gave it life, it now lies in the cold repose of a dead person, its door closed tight and its window staring fixedly like the lips and eye of a corpse:

Mis ojos han visto
el cuarto cerrado;
cual inmóviles labios su puerta . . .
¡está silenciado! . . .
Su oblonga ventana como un ojo abierto,
vidrioso me mira,
como un ojo triste,
con mirada que nunca retira
como un ojo muerto.
Por la grieta salen
las emanaciones
frías y morbosas;
¡ay, las humedades como pesarosas
fluyen a la acera:
como si de lágrimas,
el cuarto cerrado un pozo tuviera!

However, despite its deathly silence, its very decay hints at the sad
events it has witnessed, at a history of lives tragically cut short or
simply following their natural course towards death:

> Los hechos fatales
> nos oculta en su frío reposo . . .
> ¡Cuarto enmudecido!
> ¡Cuarto tenebroso!
> ¡con sus penas habrá atardecido
> cuántas juventudes!
> ¡Oh, cuántas bellezas habrá despedido!
> ¡cuántas agonías!
> ¡cuántas ataúdes!

For in the oppressive atmosphere of this abandoned room where all
joyful bustle and activity have come to an end forever, time has left
behind it the mark of its inexorable march. The room, therefore, bears
testimony to the cruel injustice of time, to the offence against life that
time and death signify:

> Su camino siguieron los años,
> los días;
> galantes engaños
> y placenterías . . .
> en el cuarto fatal, aterido,
> todo ha terminado;
> hoy sus sombras el ánima oprimen:
> ¡y está como un crimen
> el cuarto cerrado!

Other poems register the poet's pain at the passing of a love
affair. Perhaps the best of these is "Lied I" (11) where the termination
of his love is symbolised by the dawning of a new day. He recalls how
his beloved, attracted by the fresh and exciting experiences the world
seemed to offer her (symbolised by the morning), forsook him and the
magic, enchanted world she shared with him (identified with the night):

> Los amores
> de la chinesca tarde fenecieron
> nublados en la música azul . . .
>
> Y tus ojos
> el fantasma de la noche olvidaron,
> abiertos a la joven canción.

The poetic emotion, however, is not expressed directly. Instead an elm-
tree slowly dying of a disease becomes a symbol of the poet's soul
which flourished in love and which has sickened and is withering away
with the passing of it. Thus the poem opens with that dawn in the past
when the light of the early morning sun revealed the first signs of the

tree's disease and gave the impression that it was shedding blood:

> Era el alba,
> cuando las gotas de sangre en el olmo
> exhalaban tristísima luz.

The final stanzas bring us down to the present. The tree's condition has deteriorated and now, as dawn breaks once again, it seems to be bleeding copiously. Its pain is so great that the other trees suffer in sympathy:

> Es el alba;
> hay una sangre bermeja en el olmo
> y un rencor doliente en el jardín.

> Gime el bosque,
> y en la bruma hay rostros desconocidos
> que contemplan el árbol morir.

The sadness of the poem is tinged by a sense of injustice. A feeling of resentment is attributed to the tree and the strange faces peering out of the mist would seem to represent the mysterious, unknown forces which impassively preside over the inexplicable tragedy of life.

This sense of loss, this nostalgia for a past that has gone forever, extends even to the dead. In poems such as "Marcha noble" (19) and "Los muertos" (137) death is conceived as a desolate wilderness to which the dead are banished from the world of the living. Deprived of all that was dear to them in life, they wander about in a state of perpetual unrest, eternally searching for a lost happiness they are doomed never to find again:

> Los nevados muertos,
> bajo triste cielo,
> van por la avenida
> doliente que nunca termina . . .
> y añoran las fiestas del día
> y los amores de la vida.   (137)

And in other poems, like "Los delfines" (65) and "Viñeta obscura" (164), they are unable to resist the lure of the world and their ghosts are impelled to haunt the scenes of their former activities.

Time, then, is a fatality to which man is subject and which leads him inevitably on to death. "La Sangre" (53) is an allegory of the human condition viewed in this light. The pilgrim worn out by his long travels and thinking nostalgically of happier days seems to represent man on the final stages of his journey through life:

> El mustio peregrino
> vio en el monte una huella de sangre;
> la sigue pensativo
> en los recuerdos claros de su tarde.

El triste, paso a paso,
la ve en la ciudad dormida, blanca,
junto a los cadalsos,
y al morir de ciegas atalayas.

El curvo peregrino
transita por bosques adorantes
y los reinos malditos;
y siempre mira las rojas señales.

Abrumado le mueven
tempestades y Lunas pontinas,
mas, allí, transparentes
y dolorosas las huellas titilan.

Y salva estremecido
la región de las nieves sagradas;
no vislumbra al herido,
sólo las huellas que nunca se acaban.

The mysterious trail of blood which the pilgrim follows for mile after mile, day after day, without ever reaching the end of it, is a symbol of the enigma of life and the suffering which is inseparable from it: it is the trail left by the suffering of those who have gone before him and in whose footsteps he must tread. But it is also hinted that when the trail eventually peters out it will prove to have been his own life-blood seeping away from him and he will discover the source of the bleeding in his own lifeless corpse. The poem, therefore, suggests that the mystery of existence is resolved only at the end of it when it becomes clear that the object of life is simply to journey towards death as all others have done before us.

An air of fatality weighs heavily over the poem. Some mysterious compulsion obliges the pilgrim to follow a trail that has been traced out for him and he seems powerless to deviate from it and go his own way. This relentless forced march has become intolerably wearisome to him — he is described as "mustio", "triste", "curvo" — but he is fearful of reaching the end of it and approaches each new stage with apprehension (stanza 5). The world he treks through appears completely alien to him, a world where everything seems blighted, as if under a curse — the phrase "bosques adorantes", for example, conjures up a picture of petrified forests — and where he never comes into contact with another living creature. Man, the poem suggests, can never feel at home in the world since he is no more than a pilgrim passing through on his journey towards death.

This tragic irony of life created only to be destroyed by time and death leads Eguren at times to view man as the pawn of an unfeeling destiny. Certain of his children's poems seem to operate on one level as metaphysical allegories in this vein. "El Pelele" (27) evokes the bewilderment and panic of a rag doll ill-treated and finally damaged beyond repair by a group of young girls in the course of their play. Described as "ingenuas . . . princesas del mal", the girls then bring the game to an end by mimicking a funeral which they perform "sin duelo". Similarly, as already seen, the characters of "El Duque" (36) are called into being for the amusement of a party of children and are fated to be devoured by them when they tire of the game. In the same way, Eguren implies, man is a mere puppet, the plaything of an unknown supernatural agency which toys with him and destroys him with the unconscious cruelty of an irresponsible child.

However, Eguren's attitude towards death is ambivalent and ultimately he is able to regard it with a serene optimism which is reflected in some of the poems already examined. In "Efímera" (78) the mayfly flies eagerly towards the darkness of death as if attracted by a light, as if it knew instinctively that life flourishes in the void:

> Y sueñas instintiva o iluminada
> en la luz de la muerte. ¡Flor de la nada!

Similarly, there is a certain serenity behind the sadness of "Gacelas hermanas" (115). Opening with morning and closing with evening, the poem takes us through the life span of the gazelles and there is a sense that their death merely marks the end of one stage of a continuing cycle. A luminous aura surrounds their death, hinting, as does "Los ángeles tranquilos" (52), that death is a prelude to rebirth on another plane of existence:

> Y en la tarde blanca,
> las ví muertas en claro de bosque
> ¡gacelas hermanas!

"Un anhelo imperioso llama al sentimiento al país ignorado," states Eguren in the essay "El ideal de la muerte" (305). Death, he feels, holds an attraction for man. He is drawn towards it, like the mayfly, by his curiosity to discover what lies on the other side, by his metaphysical hunger, by his longing to go beyond the limitations of his earthly condition and to lose himself in a greater reality, by "una aspiración al infinito, el afán de conocer la ciudad nueva espiritual, misteriosa" (305). Despite his fear of the unknown, he is sustained by hope, which is like a light beckoning him from beyond the tomb: "Sólo sabemos, puesto que la sentimos, que hay una luz lejana que nos atrae a un espacio sin finales . . . es la Esperanza" (320). Amidst the uncertainties of life the emotion of hope is a reality which cannot be denied. For Eguren it is supernaturally inspired, a form of grace which fortifies his faith in an after-life. Existence, he feels, follows the same cycle as the sun which sets only to rise again: "El sol pinta el Oriente y se aproxima claro, cual caballero andante sigue su ruta de oro, con la beldad naciente y el corazón de las promesas; lleva la senda augusta para encender la hondura y morir en la tiniebla. Se aparta de los ojos, con su celaje tenue, para venir a nuevas horas. De igual el sol de la existencia traspone el meridiano y anuncia ardiente día" (307-8). Death is not to be feared as the extinction of life, but to be looked forward to as its culmination: "Debemos amar la vida para no temer la muerte, que es un pórtico de renovación: es decir: de nueva vida" (307).

Eguren's visionary poetics assumes the existence of a platonic ideal world of perfect beauty and for him, as for Baudelaire, the poetic experience is a foretaste of "the splendours lying beyond the grave". The beauty glimpsed by the poet is a manifestation and a confirmation of that ideal world: "La belleza es . . . la emanación de un plano superior, de un cielo; es . . . una afirmación y una esperanza" (249). That beauty, however, is but a pale reflection of the perfect beauty of the ideal world which is beyond the grasp of human faculties: "La belleza inmanente es inasequible, pertenece a un plano innatural. La belleza pura excede a nuestros sentidos, de presentarse a ellos los apagaría" (245). It is only by passing through the portals of death that man can gain access to that ideal world where the soul will bask in the bliss of perfect beauty. An interesting poem in this context is "Rêverie" (14) where the poet catches fleeting glimpses of two elusive "dulces bellezas matinales". There is an air of infinite sadness about them as they wander pitifully through a labyrinth of roads and forests like travellers who have lost their way, and their beauty seems to be tarnished by contact with an alien world where they have all the appearance of being exiles:

> Y al fin las divisé lastimosas
> por los caminos y por las abras.

The poem, therefore, suggests that perfect beauty can exist only in the ideal world. It would seem, moreover, that Eguren is here giving expression to an idea akin to the platonic theory of Anamnesis, the soul's recollection of its celestial origin: he projects on to the two beauties his soul's nostalgia, inspired by the spectacle of them, for the ideal world from which it was banished at birth and to which it will return only when it is released in death. Eguren, therefore, is able to view death as a kind of homecoming. As he reaches the last bend on the road through life, he is reminded of the path leading to a mansion where he was

happy in a remote past: "Basta ver la curva del camino para, por ana-
logía, recordar la senda que nos llevara a la mansión feliz" (312).

In that ideal world beyond the grave, Eguren believes, the
emotional experiences of our life lie latent, waiting for us to relive
them, like pieces of music engraved on a gramophone record: "Si en el
orden físico perduran las emociones por invención mecánica, es un
hecho metafísico que todos los actos y emociones de nuestra vida
deben pervivir en un plano desconocido; nuestros fantasmas imaginados,
nuestros sentimientos y amores de otros días, deben existir velados a
nuestros sentidos y a nuestra conciencia, en el corazón, tal vez, de la
primera causa. De otra suerte los hechos pretéritos no tendrían razón de
haber acontecido" (306). They exist in purified form, as essences shorn
of all the imperfections they had on earth: "Los amores, los senti-
mientos florecidos, la superación volitiva, el final de amor que nos dejó
con dulce pena, más allá de la muerte se repetirán, y la parte de belleza
que tuvieron en vida triunfará sobre el pesar y el final será un principio"
(306-7). The dead, too, survive, stripped of their material forms, as
pure emotional states, as the essence of what they were in life: "...
en lo eterno más allá de la vida ... las almas no pueden olvidar, por no
ser densas y espaciales. No pueden olvidar el sentimiento, pues al perder
su forma, se vuelven un amor. Un muerto es una pasión que perdura"
(321-22). He argues that the dead are able to communicate with us and
that through them we can have foreknowledge of the world beyond the
grave: "Hay una visión antelada, una transparencia que nos hace vivir la
vida de los muertos. Los podemos advertir a nuestra vera y oír en la
mente sus palabras tácitas ..." (305-6). The essay "Noche azul" (320)
records one such experience when the spirit of his dead beloved came
to him in the night. In communion with her, his soul experienced a
joyful sense of liberation which he felt was a prelude to the union of
their souls in the after-life. This would seem to add a new dimension to
"La niña de la lámpara azul" (51). The protagonist of the poem is not
merely a symbol of illusion and of ecstatic transportation: she is
literally the spirit of one of the dead adolescent girls of other poems
come to bring the poet a message of hope by giving him a glimpse of
the splendour of life on the other side.[7]

Sustained by this image of the after-life, Eguren was able to write
in "El bote viejo" (126) a poem very different in its implications from

7. In the essay "La Esperanza" Eguren personifies hope as a young girl bearing a
   light: "Pero siempre en la bruma cerrada hay una luz. Es la lámpara de la tarde,
   la niña de cera que existe como una esperanza e ilumina la sombra con el
   candor de sus ojos" (282).

"La sangre", though superficially similar.[8] A symbol of the poet himself and of man in general, the old boat appears out of the morning mist on the beach where it was swept up during the night:

> Bajo brillante niebla,
> de saladas actinias cubierto,
> amaneció en la playa
> un bote viejo.
>
> Con arena, se mira
> la banda de sus bateleros,
> y en la quilla verdosos
> calafateos.
>
> Bote triste, yacente,
> por los moluscos horadado;
> ha venido de ignotos
> muelles amargos.
>
> Apareció en la bruma
> y en la harmonía de la aurora;
> trajo de los rompientes
> doradas conchas.

The static picture of it presented by these first four stanzas – the only verbs of movement refer to what happened in the past – underlines its worn-out condition. A series of details highlights its physical deterioration – it is caked with sea-weed, sand and slime, and barnacles have eaten away at it –, but it is also humanised and endowed with the spiritual characteristics of age: melancholy and prostrate, it has been defeated morally as well as physically by the years. Brief references to its personal history indicate that it has experienced life's dual nature: it has known suffering in long-forgotten ports and the sea-weed, sand and slime are marks of the hardships which have scarred it on its journey through life, yet it also carries with it memories of pleasant times in the shape of golden shells.

In contrast to the immobility of the opening scene, the beach comes alive in the following stanzas. Birds perch on the boat, children play on it, lovers use it as a love nest:

> A sus bancos remeros,
> a sus amarillentas sogas,
> vienen los cormoranes
> y las gaviotas.

8. My interpretation of "El bote viejo" owes much to Cisneros, whose thesis consists largely of an exhaustive analysis of the poem.

> Los pintorescos niños,
> cuando dormita la marea,
> lo llenan de cordajes
> y de banderas.
>
> Los novios, en la tarde,
> en su alta quilla se recuestan;
> y a los vientos marinos,
> de amor se besan.

At first sight it seems that the boat has found a pleasant sanctuary, but in fact it is a discordant element in this setting. All this movement and vitality merely throw into relief its exhaustion and decay, and emphasise that it is close to death and no longer belongs in the world of the living. It is soon made clear, moreover, that the boat is not happy here. It is anxious to reach the golden harbours of its final destination and when night falls it goes forth on its last journey:

> Mas el bote ruinoso
> de las arenas del estuario,
> ansía los distantes
> muelles dorados.
>
> Y en la profunda noche,
> en fino tumbo abrillantado,
> partió el bote muriente
> a los puertos lejanos.

Its eagerness to set out is underlined by the verb "partir" which indicates a willed departure in contrast to the apparently fortuitous arrival suggested by the verb "amanecer" in the first stanza. Death is thus seen as something desirable, a journey through darkness towards some luminous region. Rather than bring the poem to a close, the long last line — heptasyllabic in contrast to the pentasyllabic lines which terminate the previous stanzas — seems to open it out, reinforcing the impression that death is the doorway to a world of infinite, unknown possibilities.

This serene optimism is expressed in more directly personal terms in "La canción del regreso" (196), where the poet witnesses the birth of a new day as he strolls in the countryside in the early morning. He inhales its joyful atmosphere in the scent of the broom and contemplates its peaceful calm in the sleeping, sunlit city lying motionless on the horizon as though under a spell:

> Mañana violeta.
> Voy por la pista alegre,
> con el suave perfume
> del retamal distante.

En el cielo hay una
guirnalda triste.
Lejana duerme
la ciudad encantada
con amarillo sol.

There is sadness in the air, however, for around him he sees the last
traces of a cycle which has come to an end as this new one began. Dead
moths lie beside the lamps around which they hovered in the darkness,
a fallen ribbon is all that remains of some nocturnal romance, and the
monotonous chant of the crickets seems to be a lament for the passing
of the night:

Todavía cantan los grillos
trovadores del campo
tristes y dulces
señales de la noche pasada;
mariposas obscuras
muertas junto a los faroles;
en la reja amable,
una cinta celeste;
tal vez caída
en el flirteo de la noche.
Las tórtolas despiertan,
tienden sus alas;
las que entonaron en la tarde
la canción del regreso.
Pasó la velada alegre
con sus danzas,
y el campo se despierta
con el candor: un nuevo día.
Los aviones errantes,
las libélulas locas
la esperanza destellan.
Por la quinta amanece
dulce rondó de anhelos.

Yet out of the death of the night new life emerges in a day characterised
by its freshness and promise, and the spectacle of nature renewing itself
in an unending cycle inspires the poet with hope and confidence. As the
evening of his life approaches and he advances along the road towards
death, he sings a song of homecoming which echoes that sung by the
doves as they returned to their nests the previous evening:

Voy por la senda blanca
y como el ave entono,
por mi tarde que viene
la canción del regreso.

Death, it is implied, is but a brief sleep from which the soul, like the doves, will reawaken in the morning of a new life and stretch its wings in a blissful sense of liberation. Death, Eguren is confident, is a return to his true spiritual home which lies waiting for him like that enchanted city in the distance.

2

CESAR VALLEJO

In "Trilce LXXIII"[1] Vallejo makes a personal declaration of independence:

> Tengo pues derecho
> a estar verde y contento y peligroso, y a ser
> el cincel, miedo del bloque basto y vasto:
> a meter la pata y a la risa.

He claims the right to realise himself as a human being, to flourish to fulfilment like the plants of the field, untramelled by moral and social restraints; to sculpt the inert, shapeless mass of existence to the measure of his own aspirations; to be irreverent, mocking conventional values which he sees as an obstacle to his self-fulfilment. In so doing he also claims the right to be dangerous, since the anarchic way of life which he proposes is one which poses a threat to the moral foundations of our society. Vallejo, in short, is here proposing a poetic activity which will be an alternative life style dedicated to the subversion of established values, the liberation of the spirit and the passionate pursuit of self-fulfilment.

At the core of Vallejo's work is a discontent with life as it is lived in the world around him. He scorns his fellow citizens as zombies, as men who have never fully lived, for the well-regulated, practical bourgeois world, ruled by reason, common sense and convention, is one in which men lead comfortable, insulated existences but are spiritually dead:

> Estáis muertos . . . Os digo, pues, que la vida está en el
> espejo, y que vosotros sois el original, la muerte . . .
> Triste destino . . . El ser hoja seca sin haber sido verde
> jamás.
>
> (217)

Hankering after a fuller existence, he selects, as an emblem of his poetics, Venus de Milo with her stunted arm:

---

1. Vallejo, *Obra poética completa* (Lima: Francisco Moncloa Editores, 1968), p.215. As in the first part of the book, all references are to this edition.

¿Por ahí estás, Venus de Milo?
Tú manqueas apenas pululando
entrañada en los brazos plenarios
de la existencia,
de esta existencia, que todaviiza
perenne imperfección.
Venus de Milo, cuyo cercenado, increado
brazo revuélvese y trata de encodarse
a través de verdeantes guijarros gagos,
ortivos nautilos, aunes que gatean
recién, vísperas inmortales.
Laceadora de inminencias, laceadora
del paréntesis.   (178)

She is evoked, not in traditional terms as an image of classical beauty, but rather as the image of man's eternal imperfection and incompleteness and of his eternal struggle to transcend the limitations imposed on him by life. Her stunted, or rather ungrown, arm seems to be moving and struggling to grow and become whole (the neologism "encodarse", a combination of the verb "encobarse" and the noun "codo", literally means "to hatch an elbow"), and four subsidiary images set her in the context of a whole world striving to reach a higher stage of existence: moss-covered cobblestones create the impression that the inanimate is on the verge of becoming vegetable and, echoing underfoot, they sound like stammering children learning to speak; cephalopods rise from the sea like celestial bodies; potentialities on the point of realising themselves (the substantivised adverb "aunes" refers to those things which have not yet come into being) crawl about like babies; eves are perpetually on the brink of a new day. The final lines describe her as grasping after a state of imminence, a parenthetical third dimension situated somewhere between the imperfection of ordinary being and the void of non-being. This, too, is what Vallejo is groping for in his poetry.

According to Julio Ortega, *Trilce* sets out to explore "el otro lado de la condición humana"[2] and Keith McDuffie defines its poetics as "el planteamiento de una nueva dimensión existencial más allá de la existencia actual y la proyección del poeta hacia ese plano ideal."[3] In *Trilce* Vallejo adopts a visionary poetics in an attempt to break out of the

2. Julio Ortega, *Figuración de la persona* (Barcelona: EDHASA, 1971), p.46.
3. Keith McDuffie, "Trilce I", in *Aproximaciones a César Vallejo*, ed. Angel Flores (New York: Las Américas Publishing Co., 1971), II, 119. This chapter leans heavily on the work of Ortega and McDuffie. Deserving particular mention is McDuffie, "The Poetic Vision of César Vallejo in *Los heraldos negros* and *Trilce*", Diss. Pittsburgh, 1969.

alienation that is a constant of his work, and while at first sight it seems to be a book that is radically new and very far in its hermeticism and expressive novelty from Eguren's apparently clear and conventional poetry, in fact it owes much to the Symbolist tradition. Yet, at the same time it *is* radically new, for, like the work of the French Surrealists, it renovates that tradition. It is true that Vallejo was later to denounce the Surrealists on political grounds and in so doing demonstrated remarkably little understanding of the movement,[4] but, nonetheless, *Trilce* shows certain affinities with Surrealism. What Vallejo and Eguren share in common is that they are both marginal figures who reject society and its values and embark on a personal quest for another reality. But whereas Eguren literally turns his back on society and quietly goes his own way, Vallejo, like the Surrealists, views poetry as a subversive activity aimed at undermining conventional values and liberating the human spirit. Moreover, as was seen in the previous chapter, ultimately Eguren and the Symbolists have a traditional religious view of the universe, one which makes a distinction between the material world and a greater spiritual reality lying behind and beyond it, a reality which may be glimpsed in the here-and-now but can only be fully attained in the after-life. In contrast, Vallejo and the Surrealists seek to bring the infinite down to earth, regarding it not as a manifestation of the supernatural but as part and parcel of the terrestrial everyday world. According to this concept, what separates man from the infinite is the habit of logical, rational thinking which has conditioned us to accept too readily the limitations imposed upon us by the so-called natural laws, and consequently the discovery of a new mode of perception would permit us to break through those barriers to a super-reality. Vallejo coincides with the Surrealists, and even anticipates them, in their aim of liberating the mind from the tyranny of reason and convention in order to develop a new way of approaching reality which would reconcile life's apparent heterogeneity and contradictions in a great, all-embracing synthesis. The poetics of *Trilce* might almost be defined in the terms employed by André Breton to describe the aims of the Surrealists in the *Second Manifesto of Surrealism* (1929):

> Everything tends to make us believe that there exists a certain point of the mind from which life and death, the real and the imagined, past and future, the communicable and the incommunicable, high and low, cease to be perceived as contradictions.

4. Vallejo, "Autopsia del superrealismo", *Variedades*, Lima, 26 March 1930.

Now, search as one may, one will never find any other motivating force in the activities of the Surrealists than the hope of finding and fixing this point.[5]

What distinguishes *Trilce* from the poetry of Eguren and, indeed, from anything before written in Spanish, is that it supposes a completely new way of looking at and representing reality.

Fundamental to *Trilce* is the concept of the absurd. Vallejo sees all our complacent assumptions of a rationally ordered universe belied and made a nonsense of by a reality that is absurdly irrational, disordered and chaotic. In poem XXXVI awareness of the absurd forces itself upon him in the form of the inexplicable sensation that his little finger is superfluous or out of place. The fact that he should have five fingers rather than four or three strikes him as evidence of life's arbitrary nature rather than of a meaningful order, and he can come to terms with his irritation only by recognising that in the everyday world life is like that:

> Tal siento ahora el meñique
> demás en la siniestra. Lo veo y creo
> no debe serme, o por lo menos que está
> en sitio donde no debe.
> Y me inspira rabia y me azarea
> y no hay cómo salir de él, sino haciendo
> la cuenta de que hoy es jueves. (178)

However, the concept of the absurd is an ambivalent one, for Vallejo is convinced that the apparently senseless chaos of life conceals some unifying principle which harmonises all the conflicting and contradictory elements of existence. This unifying principle, which seems an absurdity from a rational viewpoint since it confounds our logic and our conventional notions of order, is for Vallejo the only true reality. For it is only in the contemplation of its authentic harmony that he can go beyond the limitations and imperfections of the everyday world and satisfy his spiritual hunger in an ecstatic state of plenitude:

> Absurdo, sólo tú eres puro.
> Absurdo, este exceso sólo ante ti se
> suda de dorado placer. (215)

Hence he urges us to reject conventional concepts of harmony:

> Rehusad, y vosotros, a posar las plantas
> en la seguridad dupla de la Armonía.
> Rehusad la simetría a buen seguro. (178)

5. Quoted by C.W.E. Bigsby, *Dada and Surrealism* (London: Methuen, 1972), p.38.

The order which our civilisation imposes on life is attractive, since it offers us security by cushioning us against chaos. But it is a false order since it reduces to rational principles a reality that is essentially irrational. In contrast, the harmony of the absurd, the absolute which Vallejo designates with a capital, offers us authentic security since it does not merely cover up the conflicts and contradictions of life but reconciles them in an all-embracing synthesis. We must, therefore, strip ourselves of rationalist values and embrace life in all its absurd irrationality. It is this double-edged concept of the absurd which determines much of the difficulty of *Trilce*, for to translate his vision of an absurd reality and to force the reader to look at the world in a new light, Vallejo has been obliged to develop a new poetic language which abandons conventional imagery and forms and breaks with linguistic and syntactic norms. His new world view, in short, requires a new mode of expression.

The poetics of *Trilce* is well illustrated by poem XXXVIII (180),[6] which suggests that this absurd harmony is all around us, staring us in the face, but that we are too blind to see it. It is symbolised here by an everyday object, the glass, to which are attributed qualities which are absurd in logical terms:

> Este cristal aguarda ser sorbido
> en bruto por boca venidera
> sin dientes. No desdentada.
> Este cristal es pan no venido todavía.

The glass is potential food capable of satisfying our spiritual hunger when we learn to recognise it as such and to approach it in the proper fashion. It is implied that we are unable to perceive the harmony of the absurd because we are conditioned to look at the world in rational terms and to dismiss everything that does not conform to a logical pattern. Moreover, as the symbol of the teeth indicates, reason is incapable of grasping that harmony because, since it proceeds analytically, it fragments life's essential unity. The glass which must be swallowed whole by a toothless mouth thus symbolises an absurd harmony which can only be apprehended intuitively by a mind that has become liberated from the tyranny of convention and reason.

The second stanza reiterates the need to approach the glass in the proper fashion. If we attempt to devour it, its sharp contours and hard exterior will hurt our mouths, but if we take it gently it will dissolve in

6. My interpretation of this poem differs from that of Eduardo Neale-Silva for whom the glass is a symbol of the new revolutionary ideology. See *César Vallejo en su fase trílcica* (Madison: Univ. of Wisconsin Press, 1975), pp.51-65.

the mouth into a soft, sweet syrup that slides down easily:

> Hiere cuando lo fuerzan
> y ya no tiene cariños animales.
> Mas si se le apasiona, se melaría
> y tomaría la horma de los sustantivos
> que se adjetivan de brindarse.

The symbol is enriched by the analogy of a woman waiting to give herself in love. If we attempt to take the glass by force, it will grow tense and hard, refuse to yield, fight back like a woman defending herself against rape. But when wooed lovingly, it loses its hardness, grows soft and sweet and gives itself willingly. Here again it is suggested that reason is inadequate for the task of apprehending the unifying principle, since the rational mind seeks to dominate reality, bend it to its will, force it to conform to preconceived notions. Life, it is implied, will surrender its secret harmony to us only if we accept it on its own terms and seek to establish a harmonious relationship with it.

In the third stanza the symbol of the glass takes on a new dimension. Described as a sad, dejected, unfulfilled individual, it becomes a mirror reflecting the poet's condition, the implication being that as long as the poet's ideal remains unrealised, it serves only to remind him of his present dissatisfied incompleteness:

> Quienes lo ven allí triste individuo
> incoloro, lo enviarían por amor,
> por pasado y a lo más por futuro:
> si él no dase por ninguno de sus costados;
> si él espera ser sorbido de golpe
> y en cuanto transparencia, por boca ve-
> nidera que ya no tendrá dientes.

The poet, in fact, has transferred his own emotional state to the glass. Instead of speaking directly of his own unfulfilled desire for the harmony which the glass symbolises, he develops the amorous analogy and depicts the glass as pining away for the ideal lover who will come to claim it. Anyone seeing it in its present anaemic state would recommend it to seek solace in some casual love affair or in nostalgic memories of some lost paradise or in wish-fulfilling dreams of some glorious future. But these would merely be compensations and the glass prefers to suffer rather than to embrace imperfect solutions. It prefers to keep itself intact for the great occasion when it can give itself totally and completely, it prefers to await the future mouth which will recognise it for what it is and will know how to take it.

Thus the glass-lover refuses to be like the beasts of the field who give themselves to the first-comer, but maintains the attitude of a superior, spiritual being awaiting "true love":

> Este cristal ha pasado de animal,
> y márchase ahora a formar las izquierdas,
> los nuevos Menos.
> Déjenlo solo no más.

Consequently, it finds itself among the ranks of the deprived, unloved outcasts, the "izquierdas" and the "Menos". But it is one of a new breed of pariahs who have voluntarily embraced their condition because they themselves reject everyday compromises in their quest for transcendental experience. Hence the glass is not to be pitied but should be left alone to its suffering, for its attitude is heroic and its privation positive, since its refusal to accept imperfect solutions leaves open the possibility of attaining an ideal that is outside and untainted by the limitations of the everyday world. It is to be remembered that the glass is a mirror image of the poet. The poem, therefore, expresses Vallejo's uncompromising resolve to reject easy ways out and to continue to strive after the full realisation of his ideal of an absurd harmony, cost what it might in terms of suffering and privation.

In poem VIII (150) the unifying principle is seen as a gap in the limiting barriers of everyday existence, a secret door giving access from one dimension of reality to another:

> Mañana esotro día, alguna
> vez hallaría para el hifalto poder,
> entrada eternal . . .
> . . . un mañana sin mañana,
> entre los aros de que enviudemos,
> margen de espejo habrá
> donde traspasaré mi propio frente
> hasta perder el eco
> y quedar con el frente hacia la espalda.

The "hifalto poder" is the poet's unrealised potential — the neologism has the sense of "falto de hijo and/or hito" — but he is confident that in the future he will find a way into an ideal reality where he will achieve the full realisation of his existence. The rings are symbols of the temporal world within which man is trapped, a world where time repeats itself fatally and interminably. But the poet foresees the possibility of attaining, in the midst of time itself, an eternal state outside time ("un mañana sin mañana"). The limitations of the human condition are symbolised by the mirror which reflects the poet's external and inauthentic self (his front) and everyday existence which is but the echo of the ideal existence he longs for. But the poet has faith in his ability one day to penetrate the mirror, to overcome these limitations and reach the absurd dimension where all contradictions are resolved in a new unity. The image of the poet's front facing in towards the back is yet another absurd, disconcerting image which translates a state where the laws of the everyday world are confounded.

The image of the gap recurs in poem XXXVI (178),[7] this time identified with woman's sex:

> Pugnamos insertarnos por un ojo de aguja,
> enfrentados, a las ganadas.
> Amoniácase casi el cuarto ángulo del círculo.
> ¡Hembra se continúa el macho, a raíz
> de probables senos, y precisamente
> a raíz de cuanto no florece!

The opening lines evoke the emotional and physical straining of the sexual act as the male seeks to penetrate the female. But this straining is also a mutual striving to pass through the eye of a needle, to penetrate the barriers of ordinary existence, to an absurd, impossible dimension beyond, where all limitations are overcome and all contradictions resolved. In the third line this dimension is already glimpsed in the image of the circle beginning to be squared. In the following lines it is attained. The lovers ascend to a transcendental reality in which they become fused in a new unity, and their fulfilment derives from a non-carnal pleasure ("probables senos"), from having attained a state where nothing flourishes, a state free from the imperfections and limitations of the day-to-day world. The sense of the stanza is reinforced by its structure. A progression towards a climax ("Pugnamos . . . Amoniácase casi . . . se continúa") builds up an impression of the lovers' ascent to their orgasm, which is prolonged by the enjambment of the final lines.

Later in the poem it becomes clear that the lovers' striving to find unity through sex is a metaphor of a universal phenomenon. All the apparent chaos around us, it is suggested, is really a manifestation of the struggle of all the contradictory and conflicting elements in life to converge on a centre and squeeze through the unifying gap, something in the manner of the waters of a whirlpool:

> ¡Intervenid en el conflicto
> de puntas que se disputan
> en la más torionda de las justas
> el salto por el ojo de la aguja!

Hence to experience the spiritual orgasm of unity, we must discard

---

7. Jean Franco advances an interpretation of this poem which is diametrically opposed to mine and to the whole argument of this chapter. For her the poem represents a demystification of poetry. See *César Vallejo. The Dialectics of Poetry and Silence* (Cambridge: Cambridge Univ. Press, 1976), pp.86-93.

reason and common sense and plunge into the disorderly, conflictive mess of life. For it is only by so doing that we can pass through the eye of the needle, penetrate beyond the barriers of the rational world, make the leap into the absurd ideal dimension where chaos falls into place and acquires an order.

The poem just examined has the form of an invocation to the reader. If in *Trilce* Vallejo is a spiritual recluse embarked on a personal quest for transcendental experience, he also adopts the role of spiritual guide to his fellow men, pointing out to them the path they must follow if they wish to enrich their lives. In poem XLV (187) he assumes this same role to advise the reader that to be confronted with the absurdity of his condition is not something to be bemoaned:

> Y si así diéramos las narices
> en el absurdo,
> nos cubriremos con el oro de no tener nada,
> y empollaremos el ala aún no nacida
> de la noche, hermana
> de esta ala huérfana del día,
> que a fuerza de ser una ya no es ala.

To become aware of the absurd, to recognise the apparently senseless chaos to which we are normally blinded by the complacent assumptions of our civilisation, is something positive. To have nothing, to liberate ourselves from false values, is to draw closer to the truth, is the first step towards discovering a new and satisfying reality. The orphaned wing of the day, which since it is only one cannot enable us to fly, is the image of the unrealised potential of man trapped in the everyday world where he is atrophied by the rational, materialistic values of our civilisation. By embracing the absurd, by taking cognizance of life's essential irrationality, we can hatch the other wing, the wing of the night, which, complementing the other, will enable us to rise above the limits of the everyday world to a higher reality where we will be spiritually fulfilled.

The poet's pursuit of his harmonious vision thus involves a process of purification, since, like the mystic, he must first of all liberate himself from the world's values in order to draw closer to ultimate reality. His is a heroic quest, since this purification obliges him to face chaos naked, without the comfort and protection of the values men normally live by. Thus, he urges us to abandon ourselves to chaos, embracing the condition of unprotected orphans:

> Ceded al nuevo impar
> potente de orfandad!   (178)

The term "impar", designating that which lies outside normal concepts of order, is ambivalent, for it refers to both the chaos of life and the absurd ideal dimension. The former is therefore also potent in a positive sense, since it is through confrontation with it that the second state may be reached.

The vision of harmony, then, is wrested from chaos at the cost of pain and suffering. Poem LXXIII (215) opens with a cry of pain uttered by the poet:

> Ha triunfado otro ay. La verdad está allí.
> Y quien tal actúa ¿no va a saber
> amaestrar excelentes dijitígrados
> para el ratón? ¿Sí ... No ...?

The truth, he says, lies in that cry, for it is experience of suffering that equips him to grasp life's secret harmony. The unifying principle is like the mouse, something elusive which has to be approached stealthily, but Vallejo claims to be capable of training cats to catch it. By withdrawing from the world and its comfortable values to face life in the raw, the poet gets closer to the heart of things, and in his solitary and painful confrontation with naked reality he goes through a process of initiation, sharpening his faculties and refining his sensibilities till he becomes capable of apprehending life's hidden harmony. Thus, after a second cry of pain, the poet's suffering, suddenly and almost magically, transforms itself into ecstasy; the pure waters of fulfilment flow from his pain as by the scientific process of exosmosis; and he finds himself at the pole of self-realisation, a transcendental state where at the same time he feels himself at one with the whole world:

> Ha triunfado otro ay y contra nadie.
> Oh exósmosis de agua químicamente pura.
> Ah míos australes. Oh nuestros divinos.

If the poems already examined propose the harmony of the absurd as the goal of Vallejo's poetics, poem I (143) is a dramatisation of the poetic experience, of the moment of epiphany when the poet captures that harmony.[8] In the opening stanza the poet feels his vision of harmony coming on and protests against the din going on around him which threatens to dissolve that vision:

8. According to André Coyné (*Aproximaciones*, II, 109-111) and G.G. Wing (*Revista Hispánica Moderna*, 3 [1969], 268-274), this poem expresses the sense of menace felt by a man interrupted in the act of defecation. Neale-Silva (op.cit., pp.27-41) interprets it as a protest against those who seek to muzzle the artist and condemn his work without understanding it. My interpretation differs from these, though it incorporates some observations made by Neale-Silva and is similar to that of Keith McDuffie in the article previously mentioned.

> Quién hace tanta bulla, y ni deja
> testar las islas que van quedando.

The islands are fragmented intuitions of a hidden order which detach themselves from the formless flux of life and coalesce in his mind. The poet wishes the islands to be allowed to testify, he wishes his vision to make its presence felt above the din which threatens to submerge it. The ambiguous syntax of the second line and the ambiguity of the verb "testar" permit a second, complementary interpretation: he also wishes to bequeath these islands, to give his vision to the world in poetic form.

In the second stanza the poet appeals for a respite from the noise, for some consideration for his need for privacy to concentrate on his vision, since this propitious moment will pass all too soon, since the vision is fleeting and must be grasped before it eludes him. Given privacy, he will be able to assay his vision, to take stock of this meaningful moment:

> Un poco más de consideración
> en cuanto será tarde, temprano,
> y se aquilatará mejor
> el guano, la simple calabrina tesórea
> que brinda sin querer,
> en el insular corazón,
> salobre alcatraz, a cada hialóidea
>   grupada.

The transcendental experience is expressed by means of an extended sea-scape, suggested, by association of ideas, by the initial image of the islands. The poet's heart, inundated by the ecstatic plenitude of the vision, is identified with the guano islands of the Peruvian coast enriched by the droppings of pelicans and gannets. Guano, a source of life and economic wealth, is a symbol of an experience that enriches and gives spiritual life to the soul. The neologism "tesórea", by its resonance as much as by its meaning, conveys a sense of the richness of this moment, while the archaism "calabrina" (stench) suggests the intensity with which it is felt. The guano is produced amid glassy squalls, amidst a sea lashed by winds which throw up spray. It is implied that the vision emerges from a confrontation with life in the raw, with the naked reality of chaos, beyond which another existential dimension can be glimpsed. Significantly, too, the guano is produced involuntarily by the gannets: the vision, it is suggested, cannot be forced but must be allowed to come naturally, of itself.

The apparent incongruity in this poem between the quasi-mystical experience described and the earthy symbolism used to describe it seems to represent a satire of the traditional etherealness of the visionary poetics and an attempt to bring it down from the clouds. Breaking with the convention whereby the visionary experience transports us beyond the earth to some celestial region, the poem presents it as an experience which increases our awareness of the world around us, making us feel the substance of life with greater intensity.

The third stanza repeats the poet's plea for consideration as the visionary experience rises to a pitch of intensity:

> Un poco más de consideración,
> y el mantillo líquido, seis de la tarde
> DE LOS MAS SOBERBIOS BEMOLES.

The lack of a verb in this stanza conveys a static impression, suggesting the freezing of time in a moment of transcendence. Vallejo is here referring to the moment before dusk when thousands upon thousands of guano birds flock together and set up a symphony of shrill, raucous sound. The musical metaphor (superb B flats), the resonance of the last line of the stanza, and the visual image of bigness conveyed by the typography, build up a sense of crescendo. This is the culminating moment of the day when the birds' activity reaches its peak and the guano droppings described now as "liquid manure", become a veritable inundation. This corresponds to the culminating moment of the poet's vision, a kind of spiritual orgasm, when his ecstatic sense of plenitude reaches a climax.

The final stanza evokes the calm and well-being that follows the vision:

> Y la península párase
> por la espalda, abozaleada, impertérrita
> en la línea mortal de equilibrio.

The metaphor of the peninsula, echoing the previous one of the island, suggests that the poet has overcome his sense of alienation and now feels at one with the world. He has raised himself above everyday limitations in a transcendental experience so overwhelming that it leaves him speechless (muzzled) and which has taken place on the reverse or blind side of life, outside and in defiance of everyday experience. The last line shows him poised on the precarious tightrope of harmony. The vision of harmony is the prize wrested from chaos by the poet who, at the risk of tumbling into the abyss of spiritual despair, ventures heroically into a void unexplored by other men.

It is no accident that the poem just examined should be placed right at the beginning of *Trilce*, for Vallejo obviously intended it to be an introduction to his poetics and to stand as an example of what he was aiming at in the rest of the volume. Nonetheless, it is a somewhat exceptional poem and gives a misleading impression of the book. For if several poems elaborate Vallejo's poetic theory and propose the vision of harmony as an ideal to be strived after, few actually depict the realisation of that ideal. In common with most visionary poets Vallejo finds it extremely difficult to convert his theories into practice. More frequently his poetry complains of the thwarting of his aspirations and of being trapped in the prison of the everyday world by the limitations of his human condition:

> Cabezazo brutal. Asoman
> las coronas a oír,
> pero sin traspasar los eternos
> trescientos sesenta grados.   (195)

Poem LXXVII (219) is a commentary on the book it brings to a close.[9] As in poem I, the storm is again a symbol of life in the raw, of the naked reality of chaos out of which emerges the life-giving experience of the vision, symbolised by the rain:

> Graniza tanto, como para que yo recuerde
> y acreciente las perlas
> que he recogido del hocico mismo
> de cada tempestad.

The pearls which the poet has gathered from the jaws of the storms are the poetry which he has forged from such experiences in a heroic confrontation with chaos. But Vallejo recognises that he has met with only partial success in the pursuit of his ideal and his thirst for transcendence remains unquenched. He is afraid that the rain might dry up, that these experiences might come to an end and his poetic inspiration with them. Hence he appeals to the rain to keep falling that he might recuperate and build on these past experiences in new poetic adventures.

He is terrified that rain might cease before it has penetrated him to the core and completely saturated him:

> ¿Hasta dónde me alcanzará esta lluvia?
> Temo me quede con algún flanco seco
> temo que ella se vaya, sin haberme probado
> en las sequías de increíbles cuerdas vocales,
> por las que,
> para dar armonía,
> hay siempre que subir ¡nunca bajar!
> ¿No subimos acaso para abajo?

For in the depths of his being there lie "incredible vocal chords", dry and as yet untried, which require to be moistened by the rain before

9. My interpretation of this poem coincides with that of Ortega (*Aproximaciones*, II, 171-177).

they can fulfil their function of celebrating the harmony of the absurd, a harmony which at one and the same time signifies a transcending of self and a descent to the depths of self, a harmony which simultaneously overcomes contradictions and embraces them. These vocal chords are a symbol of the poet's potential which as yet has only been partially realised and which can only be fully realised through fresh contact with the absurd ideal dimension. Hence the last line of the poem and the book presents the poet as an arid coast cut off from the sea, and he appeals to the rain to keep falling till he is saturated and submerged in the ocean, till he loses his separate identity in the universal harmony:

Canta, lluvia, en la costa aun sin mar!

In the last poem of *Trilce* Vallejo finds himself in the position of an explorer who has reached the fringes of an undiscovered land and glimpsed something of its marvels but as yet has been unable to penetrate into its interior. Coming at the end of the volume, the poem indicates that his quest for transcendental experience will be carried over into his later work. In fact Vallejo was to abandon this type of poetry. In the uncertain political and economic climate of the 1920s he underwent a crisis of conscience which led him to re-examine his previous attitudes. For while the poetics of *Trilce* was revolutionary in the sense that it implied an assault on established values and was directed towards the spiritual liberation of man, he now began to question whether such a liberation was feasible without the previous social emancipation of the masses and to ask himself if his solitary activity did not represent a betrayal of the millions of human beings who were the victims of social injustice. Implicit in his condemnation of the Surrealists is a repudiation of the poetics which he himself had practised in *Trilce*, and in *Poemas humanos* this repudiation was to become explicit:

Un hombre . . . .
. . . tiembla de frío, tose, escupe sangre.
¿Cabrá aludir jamás al Yo profundo?

Otro busca en el fango huesos, cáscaras.
¿Como escribir, después, del infinito?   (417)

Vallejo, therefore, was to renounce his personal quest for the absolute and become a militant communist convinced that he must channel his energies into the collective task of building a brave new world. The ideal which animates his later poetry is no longer that of a secret transcendental order but the dream of a world transformed and redeemed by the Revolution.

3

CESAR MORO

If the visionary poetry of *Trilce* was destined to be only a phase in Vallejo's career, César Moro and Martín Adán were to keep that tradition alive in Peru.[1] Moro (1903-56) was an active member of the Surrealist movement in France (1925-34) and in Mexico (1938-48). The rejection of the alienating reality in which he was born and brought up in order to assume another felt to be more authentic is perhaps the key to his life and career. Detesting Lima — he it was who coined the phrase "Lima la horrible" —, he abandoned Peru in his youth and spent most of his adult life in voluntary exile before returning to live out his last years as a lonely, marginal figure in his native city. He dropped his given name — Alfredo Quispez Asín — and adopted a pseudonym, and with the exception of *La Tortuga Ecuestre*, written in 1938-39 and published posthumously in 1957, he chose to write his work in French.[2] "¿Cómo no seguir en los sitios de peligro donde no caben ni salvación ni regreso?" he wrote to his friend Xavier Villaurrutia. "Tanto peor si la 'realidad' vence una vez y otra y convence a los eternos convencidos trayendo entre los brazos verdaderos despojos: el hierro y el cemento o la hoz y el martillo como argumentos definitivos para justificar la prodigiosa bestialización de la vida humana. / Ese mundo no es el nuestro" (133). Like his fellow Surrealists he regarded poetry as a way of life lived outside the comfortable world of the bourgeois and devoted to the passionate pursuit of a super-reality, and like them he saw the artist as a revolutionary waging a campaign of subversion aimed at overthrowing a hated civilisation and liberating the human species.

Thus "Visión de pianos apolillados cayendo en ruinas" (17), the

1. It is curious that neither Moro nor Adán seem to have shown any interest in the poetry of Vallejo or to have recognised him as a soul-mate.
2. César Moro, *La Tortuga Ecuestre y otros poemas* (Lima: Ediciones Tigrondine, 1957) includes other poems written in Spanish over the period 1924-1949. Also in Spanish is a volume of prose texts entitled *Los anteojos de azufre* (Lima, 1957). His works in French are: *Le château de grisou* (Mexico, 1943); *Lettre d'amour* (Mexico, 1944); *Trafalgar Square* (Lima, 1954); *Amour à mort* (Paris, 1957). The edition used is *La Tortuga Ecuestre y otros textos*, ed. Julio Ortega (Caracas: Monte Avila, 1976).

first poem of *La Tortuga Ecuestre*, looks forward to the emergence of a
new, revolutionary art:

El incesto representado por un señor de levita
Recibe las felicitaciones del viento caliente del incesto
Una rosa fatigada soporta un cadáver de pájaro
Pájaro de plomo dónde tienes el cesto del canto
Y las provisiones para tu cría de serpientes de reloj
Cuando acabes de estar muerto serás una brújula borracha
Un cabestro sobre el lecho esperando un caballero moribundo de
    las islas del Pacífico que navega en una tortuga musical divina
    y cretina

The opening lines denounce the debasement of Poetry by our
bourgeois civilisation. The contemporary poet is depicted as a man
assimilated into the established order, a respectable and successful
frock-coated bourgeois involved in an incestuous relationship with a
bourgeois audience, pandering to its taste and basking in its applause,
and in whose hands Poetry has degenerated into hackneyed versifying
in which worn-out imagery (the withered rose) sustains a verse which,
like the corpse of a bird, no longer has any song to it. In contrast, in
line 7, the true poet is portrayed as an ailing knight errant, the last and
apparently decadent representative of a dying breed of noble-minded
artists, who has been dispossessed of his inheritance and driven beyond
society's pale to live the lonely life of an outcast in remote Pacific
islands. But this spiritual exile is also self-imposed. Repulsed by society,
the true artist himself refuses to have any truck with an art which has
been appropriated by the bourgeoisie and instead prefers to go his own
way and to pursue his own ideals. His poetic activity is envisaged as an
exploration of uncharted seas, symbol of the dark and mysterious
world of the subconscious, and the steed which carries him through
that world is the equestrian turtle referred to in the title of the volume,
a creature of the deep representing the forces of the subconscious
which are the vehicle of the poetic adventure and which, though dis-
missed by the rationally-minded as childish and not to be taken
seriously, nonetheless generate the divine music of a super-reality. The
true mission of the poet, Moro suggests here, is not to court fame and
fortune by churning out pretty verses for a philistine public but to
strive single-mindedly for authentic self-fulfilment by delving into the
depths of his own subconscious in quest of a super-reality.

The rhetorical question, addressed in lines 4-5 to the leaden bird
that Poetry has become and sarcastically taking it to task for misplacing
the basket of song containing the provisions to feed the serpent brood

of the clock, scornfully dismisses contemporary poetry as a mere diversion providing distraction for a public obsessed with filling up time and gloats over the irony that it itself will fall victim to time since it lacks the qualities necessary for art to survive the vicissitudes of fashion. Such poetry, Moro forecasts (1.6), is doomed inevitably to die, and only then, when it ceases to be the property of the bourgeois, will Poetry be restored once again to artists worthy of it. When that day comes, Poetry, like a madly wavering compass, will guide the true poet home to reclaim his inheritance and it will provide a halter where he can at last tie up his steed and a bed where he can sleep the sleep of the brave at the end of his lonely adventure in exile.

As the title indicates, the poem is a prophetic vision of the extinction of bourgeois civilisation, and the second half of the composition evokes a future when Poetry will have become a weapon directed against that civilisation:

> Serás un mausoleo a las víctimas de la peste o un equilibrio pasajero
>   entre dos trenes que chocan
> Mientras la plaza se llena de humo y de paja y llueve algodón
>   arroz agua cebollas y vestigios de alta arqueología
> Una sartén dorada con un retrato de mi madre
> Un banco de césped con tres estatuas de carbón
> Ocho cuartillas de papel manuscritas en alemán
> Algunos días de la semana en cartón con la nariz azul
> Pelos de barba de diferentes presidentes de la república del Perú
>   clavándose como flechas de piedra en la calzada y produciendo
>   un patriotismo violento en los enfermos de la vejiga
> Serás un volcán minúsculo más bello que tres perros sedientos
>   haciéndose reverencias y recomendaciones sobre la manera de
>   hacer crecer el trigo en pianos fuera de uso

The holocaust is envisaged as the making, over an enormous fire, of a great stew whose ingredients will be not only rice and water and onions, but the various detested elements of bourgeois civilisation: the cult of domestic order and routine epitomised by the poet's own mother; the taming of nature by urbanisation as exemplified by the little city park with its bench and statues; the fossilisation of life represented by academic pedantry; the regimentation of human existence implicit in the compartmentalisation of the week into work days and rest days; the aggressive nationalism preached by militaristic politicians manipulating sick minds. Then Poetry will emerge as a vindication of all those who in the past have fallen victim to the plague of bourgeois materialism, while those who live through the traumatic days of the disintegration of a seemingly stable world will draw comfort from the fleeting moments of harmony it has to offer. But above all, though a seemingly harmless activity, a mere "miniscule volcano", it will precipitate the process of destruction by undermining established values. The final image ironically equates the "wise men" of the academies with performing dogs as they deliberate on means of renovating a culture that is irremediably moribund, and implies that the only fresh life likely to flourish on that barren ground is the vegetation which will spring up to overgrow its ruins. Bourgeois civilisation is beyond redemption, the poem predicts, and the future lies with a healthier culture dedicated to an entirely different set of values.

Just as Eguren adopted the adolescent girl of "La niña de la lámpara azul" as the emblem of his poetic creed, so Moro chooses the figure of the madman to embody his poetics in "A vista perdida" (20-21), a poem where chaotic enumeration, the absence of punctuation and perplexing surrealist imagery create an overall impression of incoherence which is particularly appropriate to the subject of madness:

> No renunciaré jamás al lujo insolente al desenfreno suntuoso de
> pelos como fasces finísimas colgadas de cuerdas y de sables
> Los paisajes de la saliva inmensos y con pequeños cañones de
> plumasfuentes
> El tornasol violento de la saliva
> La palabra designando el objeto propuesto por su contrario
> El árbol como una lamparilla mínima
> La pérdida de las facultades y la adquisición de la demencia
> El lenguaje afásico y sus perspectivas embriagadoras
> La logoclonia el tic la rabia el bostezo interminable
> La estereotipia el pensamiento prolijo

Immediately noticeable is the contrast between the gentle sweetness of Eguren's character and the aggressiveness of Moro's. For the image of the "fountain-pen cannons" in line 2 conjures up a picture of a man going around squirting ink on people with total disregard for social propriety, and establishes a parallel between the madman's irreverent and outrageous conduct and the activity of the poet who likewise wields the pen to cultivate a poetry of the irrational to wage war on conventional values. Moreover, while Eguren's figure symbolises the child-like illusion that is necessary to perceive a greater spiritual reality, Moro's poem is much more radical, implying that nothing less than a total derangement of the senses is required to attain a super-reality. Thus the title of the poem suggests that what society regards as madness is in fact the vehicle for discovering the hidden world which the eye cannot see, the marvellous landscapes which lie beyond the bounds of our rational faculties.

The poem is a profession of faith. Renouncing reason, Moro dons the wildly dishevelled hair of the madman proudly, like an emblem of aristocratic distinction, and revels in the immense, limitless landscapes which unfold before the lunatic who drools at the mouth. For the deranged mind, likened to a sunflower turning to catch the sun, has a logic of its own and, with a flexibility the rational mind does not possess, is capable of changing direction in its pursuit of life-giving truth. It designates objects by words denoting the opposite, because it perceives a hidden unity underlying the apparent divisions and contradictions of life, and it sees a lamp where others see a tree, because for it objects are not what they seem to be but what the imagination chooses to make them. Aphasia, the loss of speech which often affects the deranged, is in fact more eloquent than words, for it is a response to visions so intoxicating that the marvel of them can be adequately expressed only by dumb amazement. Hence for Moro madness is not the sickness it is generally held to be but a privileged state which has to be acquired by freeing oneself from the strait-jacket of reason, and he ends this opening section of the poem with an enumeration of further symptoms of derangement — spasms, twitches, rages, staring into space, obsessions, prolix trains of thought — which he regards as so many badges to be worn with pride.

The central section of the poem is a eulogy of stupor, the rapture induced by the spectacle of the super-reality the everyday world becomes when beheld through eyes unblinkered by reason:

El estupor
El estupor de cuentas de cristal
El estupor de vaho de cristal de ramas de coral de bronquios y de plumas
El estupor submarino y terso resbalando perlas de fuego impermeable a la risa como un plumaje de ánade delante de los ojos
El estupor inclinado a la izquierda flameante a la derecha de columnas de trapo y de humo en el centro detrás de una escalera vertical sobre un columpio
Bocas de dientes de azúcar y lenguas de petróleo renacientes y moribundas descuelgan coronas sobre senos opulentos bañados de miel y de racimos ácidos y variables de saliva
El estupor robo de estrellas gallinas limpias labradas en roca y tierna tierra firme mide la tierra del largo de los ojos
El estupor joven paria de altura afortunada
El estupor mujeres dormidas sobre colchones de cáscaras de fruta coronadas de cadenas finas desnudas

El estupor los trenes de la víspera recojiendo los ojos dispersos en
las praderas cuando el tren vuela y el silencio no puede seguir
al tren que tiembla

El estupor como ganzúa derribando puertas mentales desvenci-
jando la mirada de agua y la mirada que se pierde en lo umbrío
de la madera seca Tritones velludos resguardan una camisa de
mujer que duerme desnuda en el bosque y transita la pradera
limitada por procesos mentales no bien definidos sobre-
llevando interrogatorios y respuestas de las piedras desatadas
y feroces teniendo en cuenta el último caballo muerto al
nacer el alba de las ropas íntimas de mi abuela y gruñir mi
abuelo de cara a la pared

El estupor las sillas vuelan al encuentro de un tonel vacío cubierto
de yedra pobre vecina del altillo volador pidiendo el encaje y
el desagüe para los lirios de manteleta primaria mientras una
mujer violenta se remanga las faldas y enseña la imagen de la
Virgen acompañada de cerdos coronados con triple corona y
moños bicolores

The opening lines identify this rapture with the childlike amazement of
untutored natives marvelling at baubles like glass beads and define it as
the capacity to experience the wonder of each and every one of the
great variety of phenomena in the world, all the apparently insignificant
things which habit leads us to take for granted but each of which is a
miracle in its own way. It is a state of mind which is graphically illus-
trated in line 10 of this section by the image of trains gathering eyes
scattered in the fields by the passing of earlier trains, an image which
conjures up a picture of simple peasants staring with gaping mouths and
popping eyes as the modern mechanical marvel thunders past. If such
images seem to equate stupor with a passive, unsophisticated innocence,
others suggest that it is something which can be achieved by a delibe-
rately cultivated derangement of the senses, by a mind which eschews
reason and creates its own reality. Such rapture may be attained by
those who unashamedly delight in the marvels of their own subconscious
and, surfacing from the depths of self like sea-creatures dripping not
with water but with glistening pearls, imperviously shrug off the
mockery of a world which dismisses such wonders as absurd fantasies
(1.4), or who, by giving free rein to the imagination whose anarchy sub-
verts the false rational order which our civilisation has imposed on
reality, glimpse new and unexpected relationships between the most
disparate objects (1.12). Measured against this experience, Moro asserts
in line 7, the physical world which can be seen and touched is a paltry
place, for it is an experience enjoyed by a liberated mind unbound by
physical limitations, a mind that can go beyond the earth to rob the

stars from the heavens or forge living creatures from rock and earth. Stupor, in short, is the gift of those whom society treats as demented and who in their madness possess the master-key to break down the mental barriers erected by reason and convention, the power to penetrate beyond the limits of ordinary human sight to a super-reality and to contemplate with ecstatic wonder a secret universal order (l.11).

Here, as in the poetry of Vallejo, an analogy is drawn between this rapturous state and sexual transport, so that the experience of stupor is endowed with the characteristics of a spiritual orgasm. Thus, in line 6, the mouths with teeth of sugar and tongues of petroleum evoke the tenderness and lust of the male as he approaches the female, whose opulent breasts likewise combine sweetness and earthy passion, and sexual possession is depicted as an act in which the male claims the female's crown and assumes kingship, a simultaneous act of death and rebirth as he paradoxically surrenders his individuality and is revitalised at one and the same time. Three lines later, the naked, garlanded women sleeping on mattresses of fruit skins represent the contented fulfilment of the female after the consummation of the sexual act. The parallel also involves a similarity of attitudes towards the two types of experience that are being compared. Thus the personification of stupor as a handsome young pariah in line 8 suggests that in our society the irrational is treated with the same distrust and disapproval as sex. The naked woman of the penultimate line seems to embody innocent freshness and spontaneity which, by calling into question the values of a society inhibited by self-induced complexes, brings down upon itself the stones of violent condemnation, while the dead horse symbolises the extinction of passion in a society where relationships between men and women have degenerated, like that of the poet's grandparents, into life-sentences of empty, dreary cohabitation. In the last line the deliberately shocking picture of the demented woman rolling up her skirt to show the image of the Virgin not only satirises the Catholic Church's unhealthy cult of sexual purity, but also suggests that true innocence lies in sexual spontaneity. Authentic fulfilment, it is thus implied, is to be reached through the liberation of the irrational forces which our rationally orientated society fears and condemns.

The poem ends with a delirious exaltation of madness:

La medianoche se afeita el hombro izquierdo sobre el hombro derecho crece el pasto pestilente y rico en aglomeraciones de minúsculos carneros vaticinadores y de vitaminas pintadas de árboles de fresca sombrilla con caireles y rulos
Los miosotis y otros pesados geranios escupen su miseria

El grandioso crepúsculo boreal del pensamiento esquizofrénico
La sublime interpretación delirante de la realidad
No renunciaré jamás al lujo primordial de tus caídas vertiginosas
    oh locura de diamante

In a humorous evocation of darkness midnight is personified as a man attempting to shave his back over his shoulder and the flowers, symbols of conventional beauty, sulk at being unable to display their splendours. In contrast the beauties of the subconscious and the imagination flourish in darkness. For the dark regions of unreason are lit up by the aurora borealis of a super-reality and the sublime reveals itself to the disordered vision of the mind unfettered by reason. Moro, therefore, pledges himself never to forsake the cult of madness which affords him such rich spiritual treasures.

In view of the sentiments expressed in this poem it is not surprising that Moro should revere as a cultural hero one of history's most famous eccentrics, Ludwig II of Bavaria. In "La vida escandalosa de César Moro" (35-36) he is drawn to the latter's tomb in a kind of spiritual pilgrimage:

Dispérsame en la lluvia o en la humareda de los torrentes que pasan
Al margen de la noche en que nos vemos tras el correr de nubes
Que se muestran a los ojos de los amantes que salen
De sus poderosos castillos de torres de sangre y de hielo
Teñir el hielo rasgar el salto de tardíos regresos
Mi amigo el Rey me acerca al lado de su tumba real y real
Donde Wagner hace la guardia a la puerta con la fidelidad
Del can royendo el hueso de la gloria
Mientras lluvias intermitentes y divinamente funestas
Corroen el peinado de tranvía aéreo de los hipocampos relapsos
Y homicidas transitando la terraza sublime de las apariciones
En el bosque solemne carnívoro y bituminoso
Donde los raros pasantes se embriagan los ojos abiertos
Debajo de grandes catapultas y cabezas elefantinas de carneros
Suspendidos según el gusto de Babilonia o del Transtévere
El río que corona tu aparición terrestre saliendo de madre
Se precipita furioso como un rayo sobre los vestigios del día
Falaz hacinamiento de medallas de esponjas de arcabuces
Un toro alado de significativa alegría muerde el seno o cúpula
De un templo que emerge en la luz afrentosa del día en medio
    de las ramas podridas y leves de la hecatombe forestal

Ludwig is remembered as Wagner's patron and as the creator of extravagant palaces which he had built on the banks of the Rhine. Moro evidently had scant sympathy for Wagner, not only because the romantic sentimentality of his operas was little to his taste, but because he saw in him the epitome of the bourgeois artist idolised by and living off rich patrons. On the other hand, he was greatly attracted by the eccentric Ludwig, who lived in a private world of fantasy which he transformed into reality in the shape of fairy-tale castles. For Moro, therefore, it is the patron and not the artist who was the true genius. Wagner, in his view, merely basks in Ludwig's reflected glory, and hence lines 7-8 humorously portray him as an effigy on the king's tomb, a little guard dog watching over his master's remains and gnawing on the bone of glory tossed to him by his patron. In contrast, Ludwig, who lived fantasy as reality, is venerated by the poet as a spiritual forefather. Like the eccentric king, Moro asserts his determination to lead a life dictated not by reason or convention but by his own inner impulses, a life style which, the title indicates, will shock and scandalise bourgeois society.[3]

Hence the poem opens with Moro's imperious wish to get away from the comfortable, insulated society of the bourgeois into the "sitios de peligro", the unprotected world of storm clouds and gathering darkness, and to lose his being in the storms and rains of life. Darkness and storm clouds are, of course, symbolic of the irrational forces which terrify the bourgeois. But behind those clouds, on the edge of that darkness, fall the life-giving rains of the spiritual fulfilment which can only come from intense emotional involvement in existence. This is the reality which reveals itself to lovers when they abandon the strongholds of bourgeois morality whose icy frigidity chills the blood in the veins. Authentic, soul-fulfilling experience is to be arrived at only by submerging oneself in the irrational, and, therefore, Moro proclaims the urgency of sullying the icy purity of bourgeois morality and of cutting the bridges leading back into its protective towers.

Moro's pilgrimage to Ludwig's tomb takes the symbolic form of a descent into the depths of his own subconscious. In the fantastic landscape around the tomb rains fall which regenerate the soul by purifying it of the contamination of bourgeois society. The relapsed sea-horses whose horns are like the trolleys of tram-cars symbolise the corruption of the elemental by a mechanistic civilisation, while the murderers who prowl the sublime terrace of the apparitions are an embodiment of society's hostility to the irrational, but in the depths of the subconscious

---

3. For a biography of Ludwig, see Wilfrid Blunt, *The Dream King. Ludwig II of Bavaria* (London: Hamish Hamilton, 1970). Blunt's book seems to confirm the observations made in this paragraph. In his relations with Ludwig Wagner behaved in a shamelessly mercenary and materialistic manner. Ludwig appears to have been a dreamer incapable of adapting to the demands of public life. All his life he sought a means of expression of his own inner world and he found it, first by helping Wagner to stage his operas and later by constructing his fantastic castles.

the purifying rains rust those false head-pieces and route the assassins who would stifle the marvels which manifest themselves there. Lines 12-15 present the fantastic landscape of the subconscious as a dark, frightening place fraught with dangers, a forest full of shocking symbols, such as calves with elephantine heads in the manner of grotesque Babylonian idols. For such it appears to the apprehensive bourgeois. But for Moro the realm of the subconscious is what the countryside is to Fray Luis de Léon in "Vida retirada". Like the "pocos sabios/que en el mundo han sido" of the Spanish mystic, the "raros pasantes" who enter there discover the secret of the fulfilling life and, their eyes opened for the first time, wander about intoxicated by the marvellous visions they behold. The anonymous personage addressed in line 16 is Poetry, an ineffable super-reality, which makes its earthly appearance in the subconscious, giving birth to a river which cleanses the soul and sweeps away the vestiges of the day-light world of reason, seen as a false piling-up of medals and sponges and cross-bows, symbols of a civilisation which saps men's energies in the pursuit of war and empty glory. In the final lines of this section the temple of a new Surrealist art emerges out of the decaying forest around Ludwig's tomb — that is, out of the subconscious which was his domain and which our civilisation has neglected — and presents itself to the hostile light of the rational world. The dome of this temple has the shape of a female breast and there a winged bull joyfully sucks, and by means of this image it is implied that the new Surrealist art, born of the subconscious, is one which fulfils man's total being, nourishing him in body and in soul by affording him a simultaneous sense of transcendence and physical well-being.

Moro goes on to reiterate his desire to lose his being in the realm of the subconscious, to abandon himself to the irrational forces which bourgeois society fears as a menace:

Dispérsame en el vuelo de los caballos migratorios
En al aluvión de escorias coronando el volcán longevo del día
En la visión aterradora que persigue al hombre al acercarse la hora
    entre todas pasmosa del mediodía
Cuando las bailarinas hirvientes están a punto de ser decapitadas
Y el hombre palidece en la sospecha pavorosa de la aparición defi-
    nitiva trayendo entre los dientes el oráculo legible como sigue:
"Una navaja sobre un caldero atraviesa un cepillo de cerdas
de dimensión ultrasensible; a la proximidad del día las cerdas se
alargan hasta tocar el crepúsculo; cuando la noche se acerca las
cerdas se transforman en una lechería de apariencia modesta y
campesina. Sobre la navaja vuela un halcón devorando un enigma
en forma de condensación de vapor; a veces es un cesto colmado
de ojos de animales y de cartas de amor llenas con una sola letra;

otras veces un perro laborioso devora una cabaña iluminada por dentro. La obscuridad envolvente puede interpretarse como una ausencia de pensamiento provocada por la proximidad invisible de un estanque subterráneo habitado por tortugas de primera magnitud".

The idea that poetry is a subversive activity is brought out once again by a series of images evoking a picture of destruction: horses fleeing in panic; the piled-up debris of capitalism — a society based on practical, positivistic values, identified here with daytime — which, like a long-lived volcano, is slowly annihilating itself; the terrifying apocalyptic vision which haunts modern-day rational man.[4] In that vision an oracle speaks to man. After a series of incongruent images, it announces an all-enveloping darkness, the plunging of the world into the night of unreason. Agents of that darkness are giant turtles, primitive creatures on earth before man and unsullied by civilisation. Here, as in the first poem examined, they represent the forces of the subconscious which will provoke "una ausencia de pensamiento", the extinction of rational thought. What is being implied, it seems, is that each poetic experience, each descent into the subconscious, effectively, if only temporarily, abolishes the rational world and by undermining the values on which our civilisation is based, foreshadows and prepares for the eventual total extinction of that civilisation.

In the final lines Moro's pilgrimage to Ludwig's tomb, his excursion into his own subconscious, ends in a triumphant moment of epiphany:

El viento se levanta sobre la tumba real
Luis II de Baviera despierta entre los escombros del mundo
Y sale a visitarme trayendo a través del bosque circundante
Un tigre moribundo
Los árboles vuelan a ser semillas y el bosque desaparece
Y se cubre de niebla rastrera
Miríadas de insectos ahora en libertad ensordecen el aire
Al paso de los dos más hermosos tigres del mundo

An apocalyptic wind sweeps over a world reduced to ruins and, rising from the grave, Ludwig comes to the poet leading a moribund tiger, symbol both of a natural harmony which our civilisation has all but totally destroyed and of the human spirit atrophied by reason. At that

4. This vision occurs "al acercarse la hora entre todas pasmosa del mediodía". Associating day-light with reason, Moro always speaks with detestation of midday, the moment when the sun reaches its zenith. What the image seems to imply in the context of the poem is that civilisations, like nature, pass through cycles and that in the very age when positivistic values have established their supremacy men have already begun to fear the decline of the civilisation based on those values.

moment history is abolished, the world reverts to its primeval origins, and the deafening buzz of the insects swarming over prehistoric swamplands celebrates freedom from unnatural restraints and the recovery of an original state of unity. The spirits of the two soul-mates, Ludwig and Moro, come together in communion and, restored to wholeness and harmony with their environment, stalk the world in unison in the shape of two beautiful tigers. Thus the poetic experience heals the scision between man and his universe and, if only momentarily, affords the poet the unmitigated joy of being at one with a world which is a harmonious whole.

Most of the thirteen poems which make up *La Tortuga Ecuestre* are love poems. Apparently conventional, they do not, in fact, refer to a real amorous experience but tell the story of Moro's passionate love affair with Poetry, personified as a woman.[5] Gustavo Adolfo Bécquer, in "Rima I",[6] speaks of Poetry as a secret universal harmony of which his poems are but an incomplete expression:

> Yo sé un himno gigante y extraño
> que anuncia en la noche del alma una aurora,
> y estas páginas son de ese himno
> cadencias que el aire dilata en las sombras.

Similarly, for Moro Poetry is an ineffable super-reality imperfectly grasped in the act of poetic creation. *La Tortuga Ecuestre* draws an analogy between love and the poetic activity in which the poet pursues this elusive super-reality with the passion of a lover and, capturing it by means of the imagination, experiences a fulfilment as complete and intense as that associated with love. Poetry, the Beloved, appears as a phantom conjured up by the poet's imagination to fill him with ecstasy and transform existence in a qualitatively eternal moment:

> Apareces
> La vida es cierta
> . . . tus pies transitan
> Abriendo huellas indelebles
> Donde puede leerse la historia del mundo
> Y el porvenir del universo
> Y ese ligarse luminoso de mi vida
> A tu existencia.   (26-27)

5. Though Moro is known to have been a homosexual, I can find in the texts no evidence to justify the assertion that the poems of *La Tortuga Ecuestre* are a celebration of homosexuality. See *The Scandalous Life of César Moro in his own words*, trans. Philip Ward (New York-Cambridge: The Oleander Press, 1976), p.3.
6. Gustavo Adolfo Bécquer, *Rimas* (Salamanca: Anaya, 1971), p.41.

As the personification of the other side of life, the Lady Poetry usually appears as an ethereal figure whose domain is the night. Thus, in "Oh furor el alba se desprende de tus labios" (23-24), she comes to the poet while the city is asleep, gliding on clouds and breath to knock at his window and beckon him to her:

Vuelves en la nube y en el aliento
Sobre la ciudad dormida
Golpeas a mi ventana sobre el mar
A mi ventana sobre el sol y la luna
A mi ventana de nubes
A mi ventana de senos sobre frutos ácidos
Ventana de espuma y sombra
Ventana de oleaje
Sobre altas mareas vuelven los peñascos en delirio y la alucinación
    precisa de tu frente

The window of the poet's house looking on to the sea is, of course, symbolic of the window overlooking his subconscious, a dark sea of seething emotions wherein is contained total reality embracing both sun and moon simultaneously. It is out of his subconscious that she emerges, borne to him by his own passionate desire for her — a passion so intense that even mighty crags are swept along by its swell — to hallucinate him with her presence and transform reality.

The dizzy sense of breathless movement created by the long central passage, which rushes us from image to image without punctuation, conveys the emotional impact of a vision so overwhelming that he cannot take it all in:

Sobre altas mareas tu frente y más lejos tu frente y la luna es tu frente y un barco sobre el mar y las adorables tortugas como soles poblando el mar y las algas nómadas y las que fijas soportan el oleaje y el galope de nubes persecutorias el ruido de las conchas las lágrimas eternas de los cocodrilos el paso de las ballenas la creciente del Nilo el polvo faraónico la acumulación de datos para calcular la velocidad del crecimiento de las uñas en los tigres jóvenes la preñez de la hembra del tigre el retozo de albor de los aligatores el veneno en copa de plata las primeras huellas humanas sobre el mundo tu rostro tu rostro tu rostro.

Vuelven como el caparazón divino de la tortuga difunta envuelto en luz de nieve

The passage returns to its starting point, taking us from her "frente" back to her "rostro". For so intense is her presence that her face seems to dominate and fill the whole universe. He sees it in the moon shining down from the heavens and in each and every feature of the maritime landscape, and her gaze embraces not only the whole of present reality but the whole span of time, taking him back, through the Egypt of the Pharaohs, to the very dawn of history when men first trod the earth. In her presence he seems to experience the total reality of the universe in a single instant and in the process he undergoes a spiritual regeneration symbolised by the return to life of the defunct turtle.

The following lines stress the paradoxical nature of the Lady Poetry who, though she does not materialise as a creature of flesh and blood, is, nonetheless, a very real presence. The very smoke which shrouds her seems to furnish tangible evidence that she is there and across a great distance she knocks at the poet's window without making a sound:

> El humo vuelve y se acumula para crear representaciones tangibles
> de tu presencia sin retorno
> El pelo azota el pelo vuelve no se mueve el pelo golpea sobre un
> tambor finísimo de algas sobre un tambor de ráfaga de viento
> Bajo el cielo inerme venciendo su distancia golpeas sin sonido
> La fatalidad crece y escupe fuego y lava y sombra y humo de pan-
> oplias y espadas para impedir tu paso
> Cierro los ojos y tu imagen y semejanza son el mundo
> La noche se acuesta al lado mío y empieza el diálogo al que
> asistes como una lámpara votiva sin un murmullo parpadeando
> y abrasándome con una luz tristísima de olvido y de casa
> vacía bajo la tempestad nocturna
> El día se levanta en vano
> Yo pertenezco a la sombra y envuelto en sombra yazgo sobre un
> lecho de lumbre

Inevitably commonplace reality, the fatality which it is man's lot to endure, begins to reimpose itself, erupting like a great storm to drive her from him, but the poet forestalls it and preserves his vision by closing his eyes and withdrawing into the inner world of the imagination where he can continue to contemplate reality in her image. The difficulty of prolonging the vision against the onslaught of outer reality is brought out by the image which diminishes her to the stature of a tiny votive lamp flickering sadly in a storm-battered house. Nonetheless, her flame affords an unearthly warmth and the break of day does not tempt the poet out into the workaday world, for he prefers the light which Poetry brings to his bed as he communes with her in the dark world of his imagination.

"El mundo ilustrado" (22) evokes another moment of epiphany, a moment when, as the title indicates, the world is suddenly illuminated by the apparition of the Lady Poetry:

Igual que tu ventana que no existe
Como una sombra de mano en un instrumento fantasma
Igual que las venas y el recorrido intenso de tu sangre
Con la misma igualdad con la continuidad preciosa que me ase-
  gura idealmente tu existencia
A una distancia
A la distancia
A pesar de la distancia
Con tu frente y tu rostro
Y toda tu presencia sin cerrar los ojos
Y el paisaje que brota de tu presencia cuando la ciudad no era no
  podía ser sino el reflejo inútil de tu presencia de hecatombe
Para mejor mojar las plumas de las aves
Cae esta lluvia de muy alto
Y me encierra dentro de ti a mí solo
Dentro y lejos de ti
Como un camino que se pierde en otro continente

Here rain is both the external catalyst which triggers off the experience
and a symbol of the passion which drives the poet to Poetry and of the
poetic experience itself which purifies and gives life to the spirit. The
humorous allusion to it falling from the heavens to soak the birds (ll.11-
12) simultaneously associates it with divine grace filling the soul and
puts it down as a mere prank of the elements, thus implying that this is
a mystic experience and yet is not, that it is as meaningful and ful-
filling as one but without its religious connotations. Thus the first lines
liken the rain to a window opening on to the immaterial realm of
Poetry and its sound to a shadowy hand playing a ghostly musical
instrument and evoking the beat of the blood coursing through the
veins of that ethereal creature. And the steady persistence with which it
falls — and by implication the persistence of his passion for her — is felt
to be a guarantee in the real world of her continued existence on an
ideal level.

In spite of the distance which separates those two worlds the
Lady Poetry appears to Moro as a very real presence with physical
attributes. So real is she, indeed, that he can see her without closing his
eyes, in his waking hours and not just in sleep or in imagination as is
usual in other poems. And her presence transforms the real world
around him. Normally it is the empty, tomb-like atmosphere caused by
her absence which proves her existence, but now that she manifests
herself again the city wasteland blossoms afresh into a beautiful land-
scape. Here, it is to be noted, she appears as a maternally protective

figure rather than as a mistress, enveloping him in her embrace and drawing him to her till he is absorbed into the snug warmth of her womb. The paradox of the penultimate line emphasises that this is a spiritual relationship. The Lady Poetry belongs to another world but, though physically separate from her, he is united to her in spirit. Hence the rain, symbol of the poetic experience, is like a road leading from the material world which he inhabits to the shadowy regions of the "other continent" which is her domain.

In other poems the relationship between poet and Poetry is portrayed in sexual terms. Thus, in "Un camino de tierra en medio de la tierra" (19) it is not she who comes to him out of the shadows but he who goes in pursuit of her with the imperious lust of the male:

Las ramas de luz atónita poblando innumerables veces el área de
    tu frente asaltada por olas
Asfaltada de lumbre tejida de pelo tierno y de huellas leves de
    fósiles de plantas delicadas
Ignorada del mundo bañando tus ojos y el rostro de lava verde
¡Quién vive! Apenas dormido vuelvo de más lejos a tu encuentro
    de tinieblas a paso de chacal mostrándote caracolas de espuma
    de cerveza y probables edificaciones de nácar enfangado
Vivir bajo las algas
El sueño en la tormenta sirenas como relámpagos el alba incierta
    un camino de tierra en medio de la tierra y nubes de tierra y
    tu frente se levanta como un castillo de nieve y apaga el alba
    y el día se enciende y vuelve la noche y fasces de tu pelo se
    interponen y azotan el rostro helado de la noche
Para sembrar el mar de luces moribundas
Y que las plantas carnívoras no falten de alimento
Y crezcan ojos en las playas
Y las selvas despeinadas giman como gaviotas

In the opening lines imagery drawn from nature conveys the instinctive, elemental reaction of the female who, alone and unprotected, senses herself in danger. As the Lady Poetry is caught unawares, startled looks cross her brow like light sporadically piercing the swaying branches of a tree, waves of panic sweep over her, apprehensive frowns crease her face like traces of fossils, and alarm wells up in her like lava. Her alarm is voiced in line 4 by the military challenge "Who goes there?", and then the poet identifies himself as the person who has startled her. Condemned to periodical separation from her in the far-off world of day-time reality, he returns now in sleep to her realm of shadows and such is his urgency to possess her that he rushes towards her almost before his eyes are closed. The sensual nature of his passion is highlighted by the imagery used. He stalks her with the hunger of a predatory jackal and tempts her with sea-shells and probable edifications, blatant sexual allusions and an invitation to copulation. And the foaming beer and muddied nacre associated with their respective sexual organs hold out the promise of intoxicating, thirst-quenching pleasure and of a rare beauty to be found in the mud of earthy carnal instinct.

In the second half of the poem the poet continues his work of seduction, combining images from sea and jungle, both of which carry associations of primeval emotions. The proposal of sexual union now takes the form of an invitation to the Lady Poetry to plunge with him into the depths of the ocean to sow the sea with the dying lights of passion consummated and to feed the carnivorous plants of their desire. In line 6 the assuagement that comes from immersion in the waters of sexual fulfilment is evoked as the haven a man dreams of in the middle of a storm, and a rapid series of images conveys the frenzy of desire as they rush us through the various stages of the sexual experience: lightning flashes and the uncertain dawn are metaphors of the urgency of a passion that can find no outlet; the mud track is the path of the senses leading to the beloved, but at the end of it she stands unresponsive like an impregnable castle, extinguishing with her coldness the anticipated dawn of love; she melts, however, and day flares up as they come together and, though darkness falls once more as passion burns itself out, the warmth of her person continues to ward off the chillness of the night. In the final lines the consummation of love is expressed in the images of beaches wide-eyed with ecstasy and of moaning, dishevelled jungles, images which not only translate the ecstasy of the lovers but suggest that sexual transport generates a cosmic ecstasy. Thus the poetic vocation is depicted as a compulsion no less strong than the sexual urge and as being crowned by an ecstasy which matches the sexual orgasm. And though the physical experience of love is here but a metaphor of the spiritual experience of poetry, this latter experience is no less real and, as the title indicates, no less a part of earthly reality. The super-reality which Moro pursues is not to be found in some supernatural sphere but is very much rooted in terrestrial existence.

While "Un camino de tierra en medio de la tierra" focuses largely on the poet and on the imperious passion which drives him towards Poetry, "El olor y la mirada" (18) is above all a sensuous evocation of Poetry herself, seen, not as the ethereal creature of other compositions, but as a mistress who retains all her mystery and attraction even after sexual possession by the poet-lover:

El olor fino solitario de tus axilas
Un hacinamiento de coronas de paja y heno fresco cortado con
    dedos y asfodelos y piel fresca y galopes lejanos como perlas
Tu olor de caballera bajo el agua azul con peces negros y estrellas
    de mar y estrellas de cielo bajo la nieve incalculable de tu
    mirada
Tu mirada de holoturia de ballena de pedernal de lluvia de diarios
    de suicidas húmedos los ojos de tu mirada de pie de madré-
    pora
Esponja diurna a medida que el mar escupe ballenas enfermas y
    cada escalera rechaza a su viandante como la bestia apestada
    que puebla los sueños del viajero
Y golpes centelleantes sobre las sienes y la ola que borra las cen-
    tellas para dejar sobre el tapiz la eterna cuestión de tu mirada
    de objeto muerto tu mirada podrida de flor

She is presented as the eternal female, sensual and mysterious, always promising more than she reveals. The odour emanating from her body arouses her lover, conjuring up in his mind images of sexual frolicking – garlands of straw, freshly cut hay, horses galloping in the fields, immersion in the depths of the ocean –, images of earth and sea which link her with cosmic forces. Yet if passion makes her eyes gleam like stars, her gaze betrays nothing, retaining the unfathomable blankness of snow. The whole of multifarious reality seems to be contained in that gaze, it is suggested by the enumeration of line 4, for, in an inhospitable world ruled by the law of the survival of the fittest and repulsing weaklings and misfits, woman plays the role of mother, absorbing everything to her like a bland sponge. Thus, it is implied, man is attracted to woman by the promise of cosmic unity and total knowledge which she seems to embody. However, after the wave of the sexual experience has erased the passion which beat imperiously at her forehead, her face takes on the same blank expression as before. The gaze of the deflowered female remains as passive and enigmatic as ever. Sexual possession does not reveal to the lover the secret of the eternal mysteries which she seems to contain within her and which irresistibly attracts him to her, and that is the hold which she has over him and which keeps bringing him back to her. In another composition Moro describes his love for the Lady Poetry as "mi adhesión sin fin y el amor que nace sin cesar" (27). Like the faith of Unamuno, his passion for the superreality of Poetry constantly renews itself, for he can never possess it except incompletely and momentarily.

While it is not clear whether the order in which the texts of *La Tortuga Ecuestre* appear was determined by the editor or by Moro himself, the last poem of the volume, "Varios leones al crepúsculo lamen la corteza rugosa de la tortuga ecuestre" (37-38), brings the poetic adventure to an apt conclusion. The title suggests that the appearance in book form of the poet's creations, symbolised by the turtle and associated with the darkness of the unknown, takes him out of the artistic seclusion which is his natural element and thrusts him into the social jungle which he has always shunned. His poetry brings him to the attention of the bourgeois public and the image of the lions licking the turtle's shell indicates that they are disconcerted by this strange phenomenon and simply do not know what to make of it. It is hinted, too, that the turtle is crouched apprehensively inside its shell, fearing itself in danger from the powerful beasts who stand over it. In contrast to the optimistic aggressiveness of the poems examined in the early part of this chapter, the poet here seems to be on the defensive, anticipating a hostile reaction to his work.

The poem itself consists of a series of tableaux elaborating the situation alluded to in the title and placing it in context:

En la desaparición de los malgaches
en la desaparición de los mandarines de tela metálica fresca
en la construcción de granjas-modelo para gallinas elefantinas
en el renacimiento de la sospecha de una columna abierta al
    mediodía
en el agua telefónica con alambres de naranja y de entrepierna
en el alveolo sordo y ciego con canastas de fruta y pirámides en-
    cinta gruesas como alfileres de cabeza negra
en la sombra rápida de un halcón de antaño perdido en los pliegues
    fríos bajo un pálido sol de salamandras de alguna tapicería
    fúnebre
en el rincón más hermético de una superficie accidentada como el
    rostro de la luna
en la espuma de la rabia del sol anochecido en el beso negro de la
    histeria
en el lenguaje de albor de los idiotas o en el vuelo impecable de
    una ostra desplazándose de su palacio de invierno a su palacio
    de verano
entre colchones de algas ninfómanas y corales demente-precoces y
    peces libres como el viento empecinado golpeando mi cabeza
    nictálope

The opening lines evoke a world whose natural beauty and mystery have been destroyed by the spread of Western civilisation. The monstrous perversion of nature is epitomised by the battery farms referred to in line 3, and the following line, where the poet sees in these constructions a hint of the columns of the ruined temples of Southern

Europe, seems to imply that modern technology represents another renaissance of Greco-Roman culture, whose architecture was an expression of its worship of light, clarity, order and reason, symbolised by the mid-day sun.[7] The spread of that technology has swept away primitive societies where men still lived close to nature and, by shrinking the globe and reducing it to uniformity, has stripped the world of the exoticism represented by Chinese mandarins in their glossy cloaks. The impoverishment of the world by the domination of nature is highlighted in line 7. The image of the "rapid shadow" conveys all the majestic power of the falcon as it sweeps down on its prey and that of the "sun of salamanders" evokes the great pre-Columbian civilisations of America, but the falcon is fixed in immobility on a tapestry under a sun that is now pale. In the modern world, it is suggested, only museum-pieces remain to remind us that there once was a time when men lived in harmony with nature.

Within this panorama the images of the dark hole (l.6) and the remote corner of the wilds (l.8) imply that instinct has been obliged to retreat before the inexorable advance of reason, with nothing to sustain it but the memory of the now extinct cultures symbolised by the pyramids. Its last refuge, we are given to understand, is the inner world of the artist's subconscious where the sun of reason is enveloped by the darkness of the irrational. As in other poems, madness and the sea are here metaphors of the subconscious. The pure, unsullied truth of unreason is given expression there as on the tongues of idiots. There is to be enjoyed not only the natural freedom of the fishes but a freedom from all limitations represented by the oysters who, triumphantly overcoming their native immobility, fly from one part of the ocean to another like royalty changing residence; there is to be found fulfilment symbolised by the love bed formed by the sea-weed waving in gestures that resemble the embraces of nymphomaniacs and by corals building with the feverish passion of adolescents; and there, too, the poet, his "cabeza nictálope" stimulated by the winds of passion, is able to see in the dark life-giving truths inaccessible to the reasoning mind. Unfortunately, this cultivation of the irrational forces which Western civilisation seems intent on stamping out exposes him to society's wrath. For the image of the sunset in line 9, where the sun foams at the mouth with rage as it sinks into the darkness of hysteria and madness,

---

7. Here the word "mediodía" seems to be used with deliberate ambiguity, so that there is simultaneously conjured up an image of a ruined temple in the South and of a column raised as a monument to the mid-day sun.

evokes the rational mind's horror of the irrational and suggests that the poet's activity is likely to bring hostility down on his head.

The following lines point to the violence that is at the roots of our so-called civilisation:

en el crepúsculo para familias retiradas al estercolero o en gallinas
endemoniadas
en un ojo de avestruz de trapo sangriento coronada de humo de
cabelleras de momias reales evaporantes infanticidas
en la sonrisa afrentosa de un lagarto destripado al sol
a las doce del día
bajo un árbol
sobre un techo
a oscuras
en la cama
a mil pies bajo el mar
sobre la almohada húmeda de lluvia en el bosque desnudo
como un espectro de perro de familia dinástica violenta y salitrosa
como soplo de elefante sobre un muro de piedra fina

Images of oppression – underprivileged families living on dung-heaps, battery hens driven berserk by their unnatural confinement – lead on to images of brutality which culminate in that of the lizard lying beneath the sun with its belly ripped open and its face contorted in a grimace. In that vision of the natural sacrificed to the sun-god of reason, the poet sees the hostility of society to him and his work and the enumeration of short lines conveys a note of panic as that vision pursues him everywhere like the spectre of the dog noble families set on trespassers in days of old or an elephant huffing and puffing to blow down a fragile wall.

In the closing section of the poem the debasement of the elemental strength and beauty symbolised by the tiger manifests itself in a naked humanity which, conditioned to bask in the warm sun of reason, is no longer equipped to withstand the rigours of the night-time world of the irrational:

en el empobrecimiento progresivo y luminoso de un tigre que se
vuelve translúcido sobre el cuerpo de una mujer desnuda
una mujer desnuda hasta la cintura
un hombre y un niño desnudos varios guijarros desnudos bajo el
frío de la noche
una azotea a todo sol
una despojos de aves de corral un baño y su bañadera rota por el
rayo
un caballo acostado sobre un altar de ónix con incrustaciones de
piel humana

una cabellera desnuda flameante en la noche al mediodía en el
sitio en que invariablemente escupo cuando se aproxima el
Angelus

Poultry scraps and broken bathroom utensils are symbols of a consumer
society which has desecrated the world to create a utopia of material
comforts, and the sacrifice of nature and humanity to that ideal is ex-
pressed by the image of the horse lying on an altar incrusted with
human skin. The final line establishes an opposition between the poet's
nocturnal world of unreason, whose darkness is lit up by dazzling
visions of the Lady Poetry, and the hated day-time world of bourgeois
society, that unholy alliance of reason and religion proclaimed by the
Angelus bells of noon, at the sound of which he spits with scorn. In
face of the inexorable advance of bourgeois civilisation and its de-
humanising values, the poet stands alone as a last line of resistance,
waging a lonely underground campaign for a more authentic life, and
though threatened with hostility because of the subversive nature of his
activity, Moro here expresses his determination to remain true to his
ideals with this gesture of defiance which brings the poetic adventure to
a close.

4

MARTIN ADAN

Like Eguren, Rafael de la Fuente Benavides (b. 1908) turned his back on the world to devote himself exclusively to poetry and, like Moro, he adopted a pseudonym — Martín Adán — in a symbolic renunciation of one kind of reality for another. His kinship with the poets studied in the preceding chapters is evinced by the nautical metaphor of the title of his major work, *Travesía de extramares* (1950).[1] For Adán poetry is an adventure in which the poet embarks on a lonely voyage of exploration of the other side of life, a journey into the unknown in quest of the undiscovered land of the absolute.

It is significant that the volume should consist entirely of sonnets. Consciously old-fashioned, Adán has none of the revolutionary pretensions of Vallejo or Moro and sees himself not as the vanguard of a new movement but as the heir of a long literary tradition.[2] This sense of tradition is particularly evident in three poems addressed to Alberto Ureta, a poet whom he regarded as his master and who is held up as a model of the poet Adán aspires to be.[3] The epigraphs of the first sonnet of the series (19) indicate that, as the disciple contemplates his master in the poetic act, he experiences a longing to rise to the heights to which the older poet has been transported and a fear that those heights will remain inaccessible to him:

1. Though this book was not published until 1950, various poems had appeared previously in journals and newspapers and it was awarded an important poetry prize in 1946. All references in this chapter are to Martín Adán, *Obra poética* (1928-1971) (Lima: Instituto Nacional de Cultura, 1971). Included in that volume are Adán's other principal works: *La Rosa de la Espinela* (1939); *Escrito a Ciegas* (1961); *La Mano Desasida* (*Canto a Machu Picchu*) (1964); *La Piedra Absoluta* (1966). Adán has since published another volume, *Diario de poeta* (1976). He is also the author of an early novel, *La Casa de Cartón* (1928).
2. Adán resembles Borges in that in the early stage of his career he dabbled in the fashionable avant-garde techniques of the 1920s only to abandon them subsequently in favour of an art based on discipline and respect for literary tradition.
3. A Modernist, Alberto Ureta (1885-1966) is the author of *Rumor de almas* (1911), *El dolor pensativo* (1917), *Las tiendas del desierto* (1933) and *Elegías de la cabeza loca* (1937). Adán studied under him at the Deutsche Schule in Lima.

> *. . . I burned*
> *And ach'd for wings*
> KEATS
> *De l'eternel azur la sereine ironie*
> MALLARME

— Deidad que rige frondas te ha inspirado,
¡Oh paloma pasmada y sacra oreja!,
El verso de rumor que nunca deja
Huïr del seno obscuro el albo alado.

— Venero la flexión de tu costado
Hacia la voz de lumbre, el alta ceja,
El torcido mirar, la impresa queja
De mortal que no alcanza lo dictado . . .

— Sombra del ser divino, la figura
Sin término, refléjase en ardura
De humana faz que enseñas, dolorosa . . .

— ¡Que ser poeta es oír las sumas voces,
El pecho herido por un haz de goces,
Mientras la mano lo narrar no ösa!

The opening stanza links Adán's poetics with the ancient tradition which regarded the poet as a seer, a prophet, an interpreter of the gods. Ureta is presented as a priest whose "sacred ear" is an antenna picking up the voice of the deity and the ecstasy he experiences as the divine spirit enters his soul is conveyed by the metaphor of the enraptured dove. Just as the breath of the deity stirs the leaves on the trees and creates in the forest a whispering music, so it inspires in the poet a verse that is no more than a murmur, for that ecstasy, fluttering within his breast like a caged bird, is beyond expression and remains hushed.

In the second quartet Adán pays tribute to his master as he observes him in an attitude of contemplation, his body turned towards the light-giving voice from on high, his eye-brow raised in wonder, his face straining with concentration, his lips shaping the groan that his poetry will record, a groan of impotence at his inability as a human to express in words the message dictated to him by the deity. Hence Ureta's anguished countenance reflects only a shadow of the infinite visage of the deity. This, Adán explains in the final tercet, is the nature of the poetic activity. The poet is privileged to experience a mystic ecstasy so overwhelming that it renders him incapable of expressing it. If he experiences the joy of contemplating the infinite, he also suffers the torment of not having at his disposal a language capable of translating that transcendental experience.

The second sonnet (20) depicts the poet as standing aloof from the religious systems devised by man to explain the infinite in human terms. Ureta was not concerned whether the deity was the primitive, sensual god of the pagans or the Christian god who suffered on the cross to redeem mankind, but was content simply to listen to the divine voice without questions or explanations:

> *El triste que quiere*
> *partir y se va*
> *adonde estuviere*
> *sin sí vevirá*
> CARTAGENA
> *There is no rest for me below*
> TENNYSON

— No preguntaste al dios si era el pagano,
De selva y desnudez y fuerza y beso,
Ni si era el que cae por el peso
De la cruz y el destino del humano.

— Tú escuchabas, Maestro; así, al vano
Temporal de lo real, fuiste ileso
Júnceo inquebrantable . . . libre el preso
En ti, hincada rodilla, asida mano . . .

— Alta, la pluma; bajo el pie, el deseo
Grifante, así te oigo, ya te veo
Callar, adoctrinarme de entusiasmo . . .

— Y de ti nace, identidad que torna
A sí misma . . . al cielo de tu pasmo,
La paloma explayante que te exorna.

The poetic experience is seen in the second quartet as raising Ureta above the real world and, like a reed which no storm can break, he remains impervious to the buffetings of everyday reality. The spirit which was within him is liberated and kneels in adoration, its hand tenaciously clinging to a higher reality. This liberated spirit is symbolised in the final tercet by the dove with spreading wings which emerges from him and soars to the heights of ecstasy where it fulfils itself and recovers its true identity, an experience which transfigures the poet and lends him an awesome beauty. Hence, in the preceding stanza, as he observes his master in silent contemplation, his imperious physical desires mastered, his pen poised to transcribe his transcendental experience, the young disciple learns from his example what poetry should be and is fired with his passionate enthusiasm.

In the final sonnet of the series (21) the young disciple, preparing to embark on his poetic career, appeals to his master to be his guide and inspiration:

> *Hosianna!*
> *Zur Seligkeit*
> *Mach' uns bereit*
> KLOPSTOCK

> *¡Alabemos a toda esencia!* ...
> *¡A Dios, florido y cruel!* ...
> *¡Obre la muerte su cera!* ...
> *¡Obre la vida su miel!* ...
>
> MARTIN ADAN

— ¡Tú, que sabes el monte y la llanura,
Ala espiritual, místico viento,
Arráncame de hogar y de contento
Y elévame a tu alero de aventura!

— ¡Alguna vez, por la pasión futura,
Me abatiré de tu incesante intento,
Con hambre y sed, mas hallaré sustento
En tu ejemplo a mi vuelo y a mi altura!

— ¡Quiero aliviarme, no en seguro ajeno,
Sino en el propio mío, en la mi nada,
Del angélico afán y el cuerpo humano!

— ¡De lo que me infundiste, con sereno
Estar, con atención extasïada,
Con un altivo gesto de tu mano! ...

Here the poetic activity is conceived as an adventure, an act of exploration carried out in the open, in the wilds, outside the comfortable, complacent world of the bourgeois, an exploration which takes the poet closer to ultimate reality so that he is able to float with spiritual wings on mystical winds, to achieve spiritual liberation and to commune with the universal spirit. Ureta's guiding example, Adán fervently hopes, will give him the moral strength to abandon the comforts of bourgeois domesticity which root him to the ground and to set out on the poetic adventure which will raise him to the heights. The poetic vocation is a kind of passion, requiring sacrifices of the poet in his pursuit of the ineffable, and the second stanza looks forward to the hardships which lie in store for the young disciple. He knows that he will be incapable of the unflagging dedication and constancy of his master, that he will weaken and become discouraged and fall to his knees like a traveller weak with hunger and thirst, but he is comforted by the confidence that he will draw strength from Ureta's example which will give him the spiritual nourishment to raise himself up again and to continue striving to reach his goal.

The tercets express his desire to stand on his own feet as a poet in his own right. He does not wish cautiously to follow the safety of the path which Ureta has trodden out but to branch out on his own and to seek out his own haven, to discover his own route to the ineffable reality that is the only security worth having. Each poet's quest for the ineffable must be an individual and personal one, he realises, and he can fulfil himself only by embracing his own nothingness as a human being

of flesh and blood striving to realise his longings to be an angel. For
Ureta, evoked in the last lines in the proud seclusion of serene and
ecstatic contemplation, has taught his disciple, above all, that the poetic
vocation obliges the poet to isolate himself and to go his own way, and
that is the example which Adán is resolved to follow.

The poet's anxious waiting for the poetic vision to manifest itself
to him is the theme of "Primo movimento in qualsiasi preludio" (30),
whose mood is set by the allusion to Chopin's First Prelude. For Adán,
as for Bécquer and Moro, Poetry is an ineffable higher reality and, as
the epigraphs indicate, the poem is based on the traditional image of
the poet as a lover yearning for his beloved Muse, an unearthly mistress
whom he can never possess and of whom he can catch only fleeting
glimpses:

> (Cortot: "Chopin: Premier Prélude: Attente fiévreuse de l'aimeé.")

> *Mi coraçón so fué perder*
> *amando a quien no pudo aver*
> MONTORO
> *O ma pauvre Muse! est-ce toi?*
> *O ma fleur! ô mon inmortelle!*
> NERVAL

>   — ¡Ay que te es trance el mundo y la persona! . . .
> ¡Que tú, tu amor, porfías por firmeza! . . .
> ¡Y tu inmediato yo maldice y reza,
> Y a ti, recuperado, te abandona!

>   — ¡Ay, Mía es? . . . ¡tu aliento la pregona! . . .
> ¡Tu voz la ve! . . . ¡tu beso que la apresa,
> La amortaja de sacio y de extrañeza,
> O la disipa si la perfecciona!

>   — ¿Ninguna! . . . ¡y ente y número persiste,
> Tu caudal y avidez no allega en nada,
> Y cuerpo se incorpora en que consiste . . .?

>   — ¡Que es tu sombra y tu voz, enajenada,
> Que en la Naturaleza, a la llamada
> Tuya propia . . .! ¡ay, Dios, mortal y triste! . . .

Evident in the first stanza is the Neo-Platonic tradition according
to which the soul on earth retains vague memories of its heavenly
origins. Here soul and body are presented as incompatible marriage
partners and an eternal triangle situation is evoked in which Poetry
plays the role of "the other woman". For the poet's spirit — the
"tú" to whom the poem is addressed — it is an ordeal to live exiled in
the world wedded to the body and, remaining stubbornly faithful to its
ethereal first love, it lives only for its periodical encounters with Poetry.
And when, as now, the yearning for union with Poetry comes over it,
the body, its immediate self — which when sure of the soul's submission

to its will, it is suggested in line 4, is wont to treat it with disdainful indifference and to care only for its own satisfaction — reacts like a jealous, possessive partner, cursing the spirit for wishing to desert it and pleading with it not to do so.

In the following stanzas the jumbling of exclamation and question marks conveys simultaneously the intensity of the poet's experience and his uncertainty as to the exact nature of that experience. His ears prick up and his heart gives a jump as he senses the presence of what might be the Beloved. There follows a progressive build up: his own panting proclaims that it is in fact she, his voice excitedly shouts out that he can see her, and then he tries to trap her with a kiss. The fact that the three nouns used here have oral connotations serves to remind us that it is the poetic experience that is being referred to. It is the poet's desire which conjures up the vision and in a sense breathes life into it, and it is his voice which sees the Beloved, for perception of the vision is automatically accompanied by the poetic instinct to express it in words. The kiss, of course, is a symbol of the words and images with which the poet endeavours to fix the vision. But this is a hazardous undertaking, for the Beloved is a delicate creature, too frail to survive over-ardent embraces, and if, on the other hand, he stands back and worships her from afar, idealising her to the point where she is no longer the Beloved, she is likely simply to fade away in the air. Implied here is that the poet always runs the risk of destroying the vision through clumsy over-eagerness and that he is equally in danger of being too detached and elaborate, of imaginatively recreating the vision in such a way that it is falsified.

The third stanza registers the poet's disappointment that there is, in fact, no Beloved there. There has been no communion with her and instead he remains a separate, isolated entity; his desire to give love and to receive it, his desire to share the riches of his heart and his greed for hers, has led to nothing; and in contrast he feels material reality in the shape of his body rear up as something with a real, substantial existence. What he saw was, in fact, merely a shadow cast by himself, he concludes dejectedly in the final stanza. It was but the echo of his own voice, his own desire projected on to the other world and coming back to him at his call in the form of wish-fulfilment. It has, in short, been no more than a self-deluding fantasy and hence his last words recognise that he is a sad and mortal deity, an imperfect copy of the Creator, able to conjure only delusions out of nothingness.

If the poem just examined ends in frustration, "Senza tempo. Affrettando ad libitum" (65) is a triumphant celebration of the moment

of epiphany which is the poet's goal and represents an attempt to
achieve what he himself deems impossible, to convey that experience in
verse:

> *Quo non adveniam?*
> JUVENAL
> *Cette morte apparent, en qui revient la vie,*
> *Frémit, rouvre les yeux, m'illumine et me morde*
> VALERY

> — ¡Mi estupor . . . ¡quédateme . . . quedo . . . cada
> Instante! . . . ¡mi agnición . . . porque me pasmo! . . .
> ¡Mi epifanía! . . . cegóme orgasmo! . . .
> ¡Vaciedad de mi pecho desbordada! . . .
> — ¡Básteme infinidad de mi emanada . . .
> Catástasis allende el metaplasmo! . . .
> ¡Que no conciba . . . yo el que me despasmo . . .
> Entelequia . . . testigo de mi nada! . . .
> — ¡Mi éxtasi . . . estáteme! . . . ¡inste ostento
> Que no instó en este instante! . . . ¡tú consistas
> En mí, o seas dios que se me añade! . . .
> — ¡Divina vanidad . . . donde me ausento
> De aquel que en vano estoy . . . donde me distas,
> Yo alguno! . . . ¡dúrame, Mi Eternidade!

Two constants of Adán's style strike us immediately. Firstly,
conceptual conceits (ll.2-4, 12-14) serve, as in mystic poetry, to express
a transcendental experience which runs counter to our accustomed
habits of thought. Secondly, archaisms and rare words gleaned from
dictionaries (agnición, catástasis, metaplasmo, entelequia) convey by
their very strangeness the extraordinary nature of that experience and
confer upon it an appropriate air of solemnity.

Adán's predilection for the rigorous discipline of the traditional
sonnet is symptomatic of a desire to encompass the poetic emotion
within a form of classical perfection. The sonnet form gives an artistic
order to the poetic delirium and in a sense freezes this fleeting moment
like the figures on Keat's Grecian Urn. Yet at the same time Adán
manages to communicate the dynamism of the poetic experience and
the emotional upheaval it produces. As the title indicates — or more
exactly, the instructions which Adán, after the fashion of a musical
composer, puts at the head of the poem to guide us in our reading —,
this poem is something of a paradox in that it is a sonnet without a
regular rhythm. This rhythmical irregularity creates a frenzied effect.
The poem appears as a series of verbal explosions, stammering excla-
mations wrenched from the poet by the emotional impact of the poetic
experience. Alliteration and enjambment create a sense of urgency
(ll.1-2) and this is redoubled in the first tercet (ll.9-10) at the moment

when the experience reaches its climax and begins to decline. Moreover, the indication that the poem may be speeded up at will is an invitation to the reader to re-enact the poetic experience, to allow himself to be carried along by it and to recreate the poem in the same way that a jazz musician improvises on a score. In this fashion Adán achieves the remarkable feat of encompassing disorder within a symmetrical form and movement within a rigid structure.

The epigraphs announce that this is to be a poem of epiphany, the quotation from Juvenal suggesting a sense of liberation from limitations and that from Valéry alluding to a kind of death that gives life. The poem itself opens with a cry of wonder and amazement at the marvellous experience the poet is undergoing. Then an alliteration on k and d converts the opening line into a stammer as the poet vehemently pleads for each moment of his ecstasy to be prolonged. The rest of the first stanza consists of a series of paradoxes: the poet experiences self-recognition (agnition) as he loses consciousness in a mystic swoon; an ineffable harmony manifests itself to him visibly (epiphany) in an orgasm which blinds him; he is simultaneously purged and fulfilled to overflowing.

The poet wishes to be satisfied with this experience of spiritual liberation, this feeling that his soul has emanated from him and is wandering freely in the infinite. For this is the high point of existence ("catastasis" is a rhetorical term signifying the height of the action of a play) beyond the power of language to express, no matter how much the poet might struggle to reshape it ("metaplasm" is the alteration of regular verbal, grammatical or rhetorical structure). He wishes to be satisfied with the experience itself without feeling the need to understand it intellectually. He is anxious to resist the temptation to formulate this experience into concepts. For to conceive thought is to conceive the agent of his own downfall, is to bring himself out of his swoon. He wishes to do nothing which will dissipate his ecstasy, for this actualisation of his potential ("entelechy" is a philosophical term signifying actual, as opposed to mere potential existence) is a testimony to the non-existence of life as he commonly lives it.

In the first tercet alliteration and enjambment create an effect of insistent pleading. As the poet feels his ecstasy begin to slip away from him, he pleads with this prodigious experience (ostento) to remain and to force itself upon him with an insistence it did not show when it first manifested itself. It does not matter to him whether this ecstasy be divinely inspired or self-generated, whether it is something founded in his own being which has flourished within him, or whether it is the deity come from without to fulfil him. All that concerns him is that it should remain so that he might continue to enjoy it.

Paradox is again the keynote of the final stanza. For one supreme moment the poet transcends the vanity of his human condition and feels himself remote from his terrestrial self, so remote that he can address himself as "some I or other", some stranger indistinguishable from the mass of humanity. But as the experience passes, he realises that this god-like sensation is itself a vain illusion and in a last desperate invocation he pleads that it might last. The paradox of the poetic experience is that it is an eternal moment, an experience which is eternal in quality but, unfortunately, not in duration. After reaching the dizzy heights of the vision, the poet is obliged to come down to earth again.

Adán's sense of tradition is again apparent in his best-known poems, a series of eight sonnets to the Rose. These poems, like the work of his Symbolist predecessors, seem to be based on Neo-Platonic theory according to which the spiritual manifests itself in the material and the objects of the material world are ciphers of the essences of the ideal world, so that the poet, through contemplation of the former, can at certain privileged moments glimpse behind them the archetypal essences of which they are but imperfect copies. Thus the rose, a consecrated symbol of transient earthly beauty, is a cipher of the archetypal Rose, symbol of eternal spiritual beauty, and at given moments the poet can perceive in the real rose the presence of the ideal Rose, the dazzling archetype of whose nature it partakes but of which it is only a pale reflection.

Thus, in "Seconda Ripresa" (35), as the poet contemplates the earthly rose the archetypal Rose seems to emerge out of it:

> . . . *la rosa que no quema el aire*
> ZAFRA
> *du coeur en ciel du ciel en roses*
> APOLLINAIRE

— Tornó a su forma y aire . . . desparece,
Ojos cegando que miraban rosa;
Por ya ser verdadera, deseosa . . .
Pasión que no principia y no fenece.

— Empero la sabida apunta y crece,
De la melancolía del que goza,
Negando su figura a cada cosa,
Oliendo como no se desvanece.

> — Y vuelve a su alma, a su peligro eterno,
> Rosa inocente que se fue y se exhibe
> A estío, a otoño, a primavera, a invierno . . .
>   — ¡Rosa tremenda, en la que no se quiere! . . .
> ¡Rosa inmortal, en la que no se vive! . . .
> ¡Rosa ninguna, en la que no se muere! . . .

The use of the verb "desparecer", in preference to the more usual "desaparecer", suggests that it not only disappears from human sight but ceases to be mere appearance, shedding its material shape and melting into the air to revert to its true form of intangible essence. Witnessing this metamorphosis, the poet is blinded by the dazzling splendour of the Rose, for what he has glimpsed, albeit fleetingly, is eternal, absolute Beauty inspiring undying passion. However, it is in the nature of things that since the Rose belongs to the ideal world it remains beyond human grasp and hence line 6 likens the poet's emotions to the bitter-sweet sentiments of the lover who must worship from afar. The second stanza, indeed, draws a parallel between the Rose and a clever, flirtatious woman whose desirability grows in proportion to her inaccessibility, for, just as love feeds on frustration, so the Rose's elusiveness stimulates the poet's hunger for it. The Rose plays a tantalising game with him, refusing to show itself yet leaving behind it, in the real flower, its unmistakable odour to attest that it has not faded into nothingness, an odour which characterises it as an ineffable reality which can be sensed but never possessed.

The seeming contradictions of the first tercet point to the paradoxical nature of the Rose, simultaneously withdrawn yet present, existing outside time in its own spiritual sphere yet bequeathing something of its being to the earthly rose which, personified as an innocent young girl naively parading herself and exposed to the constant danger of the pawing of the seasons, cannot escape the cruel ravages of time. In the litany of the final tercet it is implied that its absolute beauty awakens a transcendental love beyond mere earthly passion. Immortal yet non-existent, the Rose belongs to the sphere of eternity outside the material world and, echoing the mystic paradox that one must die in order to live, the last lines suggest that in contemplation of it one ceases to live in the ordinary sense to experience authentic eternal life.

The reality of this immaterial flower which is the object of the poet's passion is stressed in "Terza ripresa" (36). The Rose is not a symbol or an abstraction, Adán insists, but a reality which, though as ethereal as the wind, manifests itself to him whole and complete, with all the sensuality of an earthly flower:

'Tis she!...
POPE
Aimez-je un rêve?...
MALLARMÉ

— No üna de blasón o de argumento,
Sino la de su gira voluptuosa,
Es la que quiero apasionada rosa . . .
Integra en mí la que compone el viento.

— Miro la innumerable en el momento;
En la ruïna del redor, la hermosa;
En nada, la prevista . . . mas la cosa
Siempre me ciñe donde yo me ausento.

— ¡Sus, Los Sueños, sutiles y veloces,
Con que logro, a los últimos desvíos,
El cuerpo inanimado de los goces! . . .

— ¡Sus, huíd si la noche ya campea! . . .
¡Pero antes me cobrad, Galgos Hastíos,
Alguna rosa que la mía sea!

He is certain of its reality because he perceives its infiniteness in a single moment of time, glimpses its eternal beauty in a time-ravaged world and senses its presence in the void of everyday existence, but tantalisingly it remains always beyond his reach. As in the previous poem, the Rose is again presented in the guise of a flirtatious woman who, when her suitor wearies of being toyed with and ceases to court her, changes her tune and embraces him. The irony of the poet's situation, it is suggested, is that while he can never possess the Rose neither can he cease to be captivated by it.

The tercets are based on hunting imagery portraying the poet's dreams, his aspirations to possess and enjoy the Rose, as swift hounds which, after all the twists and turns of the chase, succeed only in capturing the dead body of his prey. For the Rose, the source of supreme pleasure, cannot be possessed and when he thinks to lay hands on it it simply disintegrates. The approaching night, skulking abroad like some wild beast scaring off his hounds, is a metaphor of the growing doubts and despair which threaten to destroy his dreams. Weary of the long chase, the hounds now symbolise the poet's faltering hopes, his weariness and disillusionment at his failure to capture a live prey. Nonetheless, he despairingly urges them on to one more effort, pleading with them to retrieve a rose for him before they finally abandon the hunt in despair.

The impossibility of possessing the Rose is again the theme of "Quarta ripresa" (37), where it is presented as an exotic flower flourishing eternally in its own ideal element but unable to survive in the material world:

> *Bien sabe la rosa en qué mano se posa*
> REFRAN DE CASTILLA
> *Viera estar rosal florido,*
> *cogí rosas con sospiro:*
> *vengo del rosale*
> GIL VICENTE

— La que nace, es la rosa inesperada;
La que muere, es la rosa consentida;
Sólo al no parecer pasa la vida,
Porque viento letal es la mirada.

— ¡Cuánta segura rosa no es en nada! ...
¡Si no es sino la rosa presentida! ...
¡Si Dios sopla a la rosa y a la vida
Por el ojo del ciego ... rosa amada! ...

— Triste y tierna, la rosa verdadera
Es el triste y el tierno sin figura,
Ninguna imagen a la luz primera.

— Deseándola deshójase el deseo
Y quien la viere olvida, y ella dura ...
¡Ay, que es así la Rosa, y no la veo! ...

The Rose can and does manifest itself to man, but it cannot be called into being and is born into the world unbidden and when least expected. Moreover, he can catch only a fleeting glimpse of it, for when he seeks to retain the vision it is extinguished like a pampered creature smothered by too much attention. Once exposed to the lethal wind of the human gaze the Rose withers as surely as any earthly flower and it can thrive only by remaining hidden in its spiritual domain.

Ambiguity is the key-note of the first two lines of the second stanza which are open to at least three possible interpretations: (1) the rose of which we are sure, the rose upon which we gaze, does not really exist at all since it is doomed to wither and the only rose which truly exists is the one which is intuited but never seen; (2) the apparently secure and inviolate rose which we see is in fact secure in nothing, for only the rose that is never seen is truly secure; (3) the truly secure rose exists nowhere for we are aware of it only as an invisible presence which never manifests itself to our gaze. This ambiguity is deliberate, of course, and the three interpretations complement one another to reinforce the central idea that the Rose which is the object of the poet's passion flourishes only by remaining invisible to him. That idea is re-iterated by the image of the deity breathing life into the Rose through the eye of the blind man, an image which clarifies how it can be glimpsed while remaining invisible. For here the Rose is equated with life, the authentic life of the absolute, and the image suggests that it is to be perceived not by the faculty of sight but by the inner eye of the spirit.

In the first tercet Adán, in a manner reminiscent of Vallejo in "Trilce XXXVIII", seems to project his own feelings on to the Rose, so that it appears as languishing in the darkness of non-existence, nursing tender feelings for him and sad because it cannot assume material form and show itself to him in the light of day. Though obliged to adore the Rose platonically from afar, the poet recognises in the final tercet that the desire to possess it is counter-productive and the harsh alliteration of the opening line gives possession the character of a brutal act of rape which desecrates the object of one's desire. Only by renouncing the wish to possess it can he hope to behold the unsullied Rose of his dreams. Thus, the paradox which torments the poet is that the Rose he yearns for is a Rose he cannot and will never see with mortal eyes and the poignancy with which the poem ends springs from the ambiguity of the final words which hint that, furthermore, he is unable to perceive it with the inner eye of the spirit.

"Ottava ripresa" (41), the last of the sonnets to the Rose, seems to be a commentary on the other poems of the series offering a different perspective from that adopted there:

> How many loved your moment of glad grace,
> And loved your beauty with false love and true,
> But one man loved the pilgrim soul in you,
> And loved the sorrows of your changing face
> YEATS

> Je sais qu'une âme implique un geste
> D'où vibre une sonorité
> Qu'harmonieusement atteste
> La très adéquate clarté
> GIDE

> — No eres la teoría, que tu espina
> Hincó muy hondo; ni eres de probanza
> De la rosa a la Rosa, que tu lanza
> Abrió camino así que descamina.
> — Eres la Rosa misma, sibilina
> Maestra que dificulta la esperanza
> De la rosa perfecta, que no alcanza
> A aprender de la rosa que alucina.
> — ¡Rosa de rosa, idéntica y sensible,
> A tu ejemplo, profano y mudadero,
> El Poeta hace la rosa que es terrible!
> — ¡Que eres la rosa eterna que en tu rama
> Rapta al que, prevenido prisionero,
> Roza la rosa del amor que no ama!

Here Adán insists that the rose of which his poetry sings is not an abstraction, but a real, living flower with thorns which prick. Nor does it form part of a platonic hierarchy of beauty in which earthly objects mirror heavenly archetypes, for its thorn is like a lance opening up a path which leads us away from the perfect world of the ideal Rose to the imperfect terrestrial world in which it is rooted. The archetypal Rose, in fact, is nothing more nor less than the earthly rose with all its earthly imperfections, which, unlike the ideal rose of poets' imagination, has not learned to deceive us with the illusion of perfect beauty and teaches us the falseness of our dreams by making it difficult to entertain hopes of such perfection. The Rose is merely a rose, Adán stresses in the first tercet, identical to every other rose that can be seen, smelled and touched. It is terrestrial and short-lived, with nothing sacred or celestial about it, and it is that tragically ephemeral beauty which the poet endeavours to capture in his verse. For paradoxically the earthly rose is the eternal rose. As it enraptures the poet, a willing prisoner of its charms, he touches in it the ideal rose, contemplating a beauty that is outside time and experiencing a spiritual fulfilment that is beyond ordinary human emotions. Thus the poet discovers absolute, eternal beauty in the ephemeral earthly rose. While the other sonnets of the series seem to pre-suppose an ideal Neo-Platonic world existing outside the material world, here the infinite is found in the imperfect everyday world viewed with a different eye, and Adán appears to be rejecting the philosophy of transcendence which such poems imply in favour of a philosophy of immanence which brings him into line with Vallejo, Moro and other modern writers. This attitude, however, is uncharacteristic, and though it could be argued that Adán is consistent in his philosophy and that he is here warning the reader that the traditional Neo-Platonic concepts of other poems are employed merely as a convenient metaphor of the poetic experience, it would seem that he himself is uncertain about the nature of the greater reality after which he hankers and that on the whole he tends to regard it as a celestial state which can be briefly perceived in this world but fully attained only in the after-life.

It has already been observed that the title of *Travesía de extra-mares* defines art as an exploration of the uncharted seas of the shadowy side of life. The nautical metaphor, in fact, constitutes one of the central images of the book and recurs in several poems. Adán's sense of carrying on a noble tradition is again apparent in "Leitmotiv" (26),[4]

4. For a full and detailed analysis of this poem see Edmundo Bendezú Aibar, *La Poética de Martín Adán* (Lima: Villanueva, 1969), pp.20-47. I wish here to record my debt to this fine book. I am also grateful to Dr. Bendezú for ideas suggested in conversation.

where Chopin — to whom the volume, sub-titled *Sonetos a Chopin*, is addressed and following whom many of the poems bear as titles technical terms of musical composition which serve to establish the tone — is held up as the model of the artist who has successfully accomplished his mission and is portrayed as the master of a well-equipped ship steering a majestic course. In "Frase in polacca per piano" (47) Adán's own poetic adventure is likewise viewed in a heroic light. The title evokes the stately rhythm of a polonaise from Chopin's Opus 53, and the opening metaphor of violins dancing on the keyboard suggests a striking-up of music, following which the poet's ship appears making its stately way over the seas:

> *Ténganse su tesoro*
> *Los que de un falso leño se confían*
> FRAY LUIS DE LEON
> *. . . das Schöne ist nichts*
> *Als des Schrecklichen Anfang . . .*
> RILKE

— Pues en el piano rïelan violines,
Singlo . . . altamar . . . un punto, la mena . . .
De mar amarga la sentina llena . . .
El tope, con colgajos de confines . . .

— Ni eché periplo o número a sinfines,
Ni de mi borda dedos de sirena,
Ni mi cantar hacia la proa ajena,
Ni mi copa y ni mi beso en los delfines . . .

— Guardéme, y no del goce, que deshace
Cuanto el sueño carga bajo el ojo
Y el olvido carena de la pace.

— Y sigo, por tü aire o por mi antojo,
Norte de azul de la infinita frase,
Que habrá de anochecerme al despojo.

As Bendezú has pointed out,[5] the opening image is visual as well as auditory, conjuring up a picture of the stars shimmering on the water. Out of the darkness thus evoked the poet emerges steering his vessel over the high seas towards some distant cape. The salty sea-water which fills his bilges and the tattered pennants fluttering from his mast-head attest that he has travelled far and long. The first stanza, therefore, establishes the nautical metaphor, presenting the poet as a mariner alone on the immensity of the ocean with a difficult voyage behind him and his destination still a far way off.

The second stanza boasts of his courage and steadfastness. Undaunted by the limitless expanse of the ocean, he has not set out merely

5. Ibid., p.121.

to encircle the globe or to follow a prescribed and limited route but to explore the vast unknown till he locates the land he is searching for. So single-minded is he in his mission that he has not even bothered to fight off the sirens who sought to tempt him, for nothing can side-track him from his course. Nor has he been tempted to divert his ship and to turn towards other vessels for company or guidance, for he prefers to go his own way rather than follow paths trodden by other poets and accepts solitude as being essential to the pursuit of his poetic vocation. Nor has he squandered his capacity for delight in the worldly distractions represented by the sporting dolphins but has sought intoxication and passionate fulfilment in the private domain of his ship. For the poet's concern is not with the things of the world and he must eschew its pleasure and comforts and embrace isolation to achieve the greater joy of the poetic experience.

Yet if he has guarded himself against all the temptations which represent a danger to his art, he has not feared to face the risks involved in the pursuit of poetic ecstasy. The nautical images of the cargo stowed by sleep beneath the level of the eye and of the careening work carried out by forgetfulness evoke the contentment and peace of mind achieved by those who shut their eyes to reality and conveniently forget the unpleasant aspects of life. Such complacency cannot be shared by the poet, for poetic ecstasy does not come painlessly and requires that he forsake a comfortable, insulated existence and involve himself in life in all its naked crudeness. Hence, in the final tercet, he continues on his voyage. Whether it is Chopin's music which inspires him or merely his own craving which drives him on, he himself is not sure, but the pole-star by which he steers his course is the example of the great composer's work, which, he hopes, will guide him towards the "infinite phrase", a cosmic harmony which will envelop him like darkness and strip him of his separate being as he is absorbed into the universal whole.[6]

In contrast to this confident optimism "Quadratura subita in preludio" (52) records Adán's despair as he feels himself incapable of measuring up to the ideals which he has set himself:

> — *¡Yo, que pude morder, remontar la teoría,*
> *Echar cartas y barcos de papel a mi río . . .!*
> *¡Mi destino, sin mengua, luna grande en el día! . . .*
> *¡Y mi sabiduría, ni siquiera rocío! . . .*
> MARTIN ADAN

6. Here, as in the title, "frase" is used in the musical sense.

> — *La Desesperación hace cosas comunes;*
> *La Desesperación hace treguas y ganas;*
> *La Desesperación hace el domingo el lunes,*
> *Y hace oler desayunos en todas las mañanas*
> MARTIN ADAN

— Qué, en sombra y fondo y denso como míos,
Garrea, anclote de tu brazo y braza,
Cuadratura de herrumbre y de sangraza
Que arráncase de lumbre por bajíos.

— ¡Ay, adónde propósitos y bríos
De seguro y mensura? . . . ¡que se rasa,
Soz, ternura de arena . . . ¡que arpón pasa,
Rozando y deslïendo de natíos . . .

— ¿A qué tu cuadratura, Mi Piloto,
Mi grímpola, mi tumbo, mi arganeo? . . .
¿Mi constancia no es la de mi deseo?

— ¿Aferrarás con número y cadena
Ni una onda mía de tu errar, ay, roto
A fermata de olvido, goce, arena . . .

The title refers us to a piece from Chopin's Opus 28 whose mood echoes the poet's own, and in the opening stanza the composer, the pilot on whom he relies for guidance, is seen as being as helplessly adrift as he is himself. A parallel is drawn between the musician's arm whose poisoned blood expresses itself in the music it plays on the keyboard[7] and the rusty anchor of his ship which drags, lighting up the sandy bottom. The dragging anchor, therefore, is a metaphor of Chopin's desperate clutching after the absolute through his art, an attempt which fails and succeeds only in illuminating the depths of human suffering. In the second quartet riding securely at anchor is equated with the harmony which is the musician's goal. What has become of those fine ideals now? cries the poet in anguish. For the anchor dragging through the soft sand beneath the ship, like a harpoon whose natural function is to scar and break up, comes to symbolise an art which wounds by laying bare the human condition as failure and suffering.

The tercets refer to Adán's own predicament. What use has been the course Chopin set for him by the example of his art? What use has been his poetic adventure, symbolised by the swell of the sea, or the materials of his craft, represented by his nautical equipment? For though the constancy with which he has pursued his vocation has been equal to his hungry desire for the absolute, his achievements have failed to match his desire. In the final stanza he asks the composer-pilot if his

---

7. The reference to the poison in the musician's arm is, of course, a metaphor of the bitter disillusionment which taints his music.

music can provide an anchor to moor his (the poet's) ship even enough to withstand the buffeting of a single wave when his own voyage has become a crippled drifting without interludes of sweet repose. The question is obviously rhetorical. For if the pilot cannot even secure his own ship, he can hardly secure that of the poet. If Chopin's music expresses the despair of a man who has lost his way, Adán can hardly rely on him to guide him out of the shoals of his own despair. And, above all, the poem implies, if an artist of the stature of Chopin experienced frustration and despair, there can be little hope for the poet who humbly modelled his art on his.

Failure is again the theme of "Dolce affogato" (71). A tone of subdued resignation is set by the title and the first epigraph indicates that the poet is preparing himself for death after a life-time of failure, that he is curling up spiritually to sleep the eternal sleep which draws a veil over all disappointments:

Arrúllase dentro de sí el alma, y comienza a dormir aquel sueño volador
FRAY LUIS DE GRANADA
Wie soll ich meine Seele halten,
Dass sie nicht an deine rührt?
RILKE

— ¿Y qué licor seré asaz dulce y fuerte! . . .
¡A sed así, que da y desdona vida! . . .
¡A ardicia y boca de voz desoída! . . .
¡A fuego que me abate y no me vierte! . . .

— ¡Ay! . . . ¡que El me quiso loor de abeja en suerte
De procurar a eterno fruición fida! . . .
¡Mas tímpano . . . témpano . . . mi medida . . .!
¡Favo que obro y resulto, arte . . . muerte! . . .

— ¡Ay! . . . ¡si no he sino poesía pura,
De glabra miel y con senil friüra,
Que flujo de floraina envenena! . . .

— Ay que no he de rendirte más que tributo
En mano inmóvil, de panal enjuto,
Cuando Su sombra ahume mi colmena! . . .

In the opening stanza a series of exclamations builds up an impression of passionate, unsatisfied desire. Here thirst is a metaphor of the poet's craving for a greater reality. Paradoxically that thirst both gives life and takes it away, for it is his reason for being but, since it remains unquenched, like the burning in the throat of a man in the desert whose croaking voice is unheard, it leaves him empty and frustrated. In the first line the poetic ecstasy is conceived as a metamorphosis in which the poet himself becomes the strong, sweet liquid which quenches his thirst as his being dissolves and fuses with a greater reality. The agent of that process should be the fire of his passion, but in his case it has succeeded only in prostrating and demoralising him and has failed to melt him down and transform him into the thirst-quenching liquid.[8]

The second quartet takes up an image with a long literary pedigree. Centuries ago Plato spoke of poets as winged creatures who "imbibed their verses in fountains of honey, in certain gardens and valleys of the Muses, to bring it to us in the manner of the bees".[9] Here, just as the bee's role in the divine scheme of things is to collect pollen and convert it into honey, the poet's role is seen as being to render praise to God by exploring the other side of life for visions of the infinite and eternalising those experiences in his verse. But Adán feels that he has failed to accomplish his role. Since, as was seen in the previous stanza, the infinite eludes him, his verse does not express its sweet harmony but echoes hollowly like the beat of the drum, and the honeycomb which he has manufactured, the art which is his very being, is a work of artifice devoid of life. Hence, in the first tercet, he laments that all he has succeeded in creating is a "pure poetry", a sterile art that is mere form without substance or vitality. What he has produced is a honey which has the cold lifelessness of withered old age, a poetry poisoned by an excessive preoccupation with stylistic effect and whose contrived beauty — the derogatory suffix appended to the noun "flor" suggests falseness — cannot disguise its failure to capture the authentic beauty of the absolute.

In the final stanza death is envisaged as a shadow smoking the poet out of his hive. When that time comes, his motionless hand — the hand which has been incapable of grasping the infinite and conveying it in poetry — will have no other tribute to offer God than the shrivelled-up honeycomb of an art which is as lacking in the stuff of true poetry as it is formally intricate. Unlike the bee which fulfils its natural function, the poet has failed to pay God his due by making use of his divinely-given talents. Like Borges in "Mateo, xxv, 30",[10] he has failed to take advantage of all the gifts which God has bestowed on him to write the poem which would apprehend the infinite in words and images.

This sense of failure to realise his high poetic ideals is perhaps the dominant theme of the volume and in some poems it leads Adán to

8. Here the verb "vertir" seems to be used in the double sense of "to change" and "to pour". The line suggests a process of converting a solid into liquid by means of fire.
9. Quoted by Bendezú, pp.103-104.
10. Jorge Luis Borges, *Obra poética* (Buenos Aires: Emecé, 1967), pp.151-52.

meditate on death and to nurse the hope that beyond the tomb he will enjoy the authentic life which has proved so elusive on earth. One such poem is "Presto agitato" (62):

> — *¡Que te quedas con amor!* . . .
> *¡Que te quedes sin amante!* . . .
> *¡Que ya glogotea el río!* . . .
> *¡Que ya se despinta el valle!* . . .
> — *Como el vilano a la luz,*
> *Mi corazón siempre arde;*
> *Como el vilano al viento,*
> *Mi corazón nunca cae*
>
> MARTIN ADAN

— ¡Que no vacua ni noche! . . . ¡que yo vea
Que en lo huero que efundo y me concibo! . . .
¡Que la tumba rebulle, mi derivo! . . .
¡Que el tumbo eche, inmortal, de la marea! . . .

— ¡Yo agonice en ti, Muerte! . . . ¡falle y sea
Siempre jamás el flaco y el lascivo! . . .
¡Mi curso, real, de sangre y de impulsivo,
Torne que torne en tu caliza gea! . . .

— ¡El mortal sobreviva! . . . ¡mi natura . . .
Modelando, eretismo, su figura . . .
Tal, que me afane como a la onda el hado! . . .

— ¡A la muerte, eviterna carne alma! . . .
¡No despojo inorgánico so palma! . . .
¡Sino torna sin término a playado! . . .

Uttered in the frenzied tone indicated by the title, the first stanza expresses Adán's fervent wish that death will be more than mere empty darkness. For he wants to witness the metamorphosis he will undergo there, to see his being effuse to fertilise the sterile void and give conception to a new being. As though to persuade himself that this is not mere wishful thinking, he insists that life stirs in the tomb, the origin of the eternal existence he longs for. He reverts to passionate pleading, however, in the last line of the stanza where, using once more the metaphor of the sea voyage, he hopes that, when his journey through life ends in shipwreck, the surf will cast him up immortal on the other shore of eternity. His desire, elaborated and clarified in the second quartet, is to die in order to live for ever and to live on, not as a disembodied spirit, but as the sensual creature of flesh that he is now. Lodged in the limy womb of mother earth — "gea" is an allusion to the Greek Earth Goddess —, he wishes life to continue circling through him endlessly as a pulsating reality of blood and instinct.

So intense is the poet's emotion that this craving that mortal humanity should survive immortal beyond the tomb is virtually shouted out at the beginning of the first tercet. Here earthly life is defined as a preparation for death, a process in which his human nature feverishly — the noun "eretismo" (erethism, a state of abnormal excitement) seems to be used here adverbially — sculpts itself into the final, perfect shape it will assume in the after-life, so that it impels him towards the grave as surely and inescapably as gravitational forces drive the wave towards the beach. Hence, in the final tercet, he urges body and soul, seen as eternally united and inseparable, to advance towards death. For death, he believes or endeavours to convince himself, is not the extinction of physical existence symbolised by the lifeless, decaying corpse fertilising the palm tree under which it lies, but a home-coming, a return to the other shore from which he departed at birth and where for ever more he will enjoy the full realisation of his being.

Significantly the volume is brought to a close by "Volta subito" (74), a poem which indicates that the poet's voyage of exploration must inevitably take him into the nether regions since his quest for the infinite can be fully realised only in the world beyond the grave. As the epigraphs announce, death is here looked forward to eagerly as the culmination of all that Adán has striven after in life:

> *¡Oh muerte que das vida!*
> FRAY LUIS DE LEON
> *Now more than ever seems it rich to die*
> KEATS

> — ¡Compás de la Bogada de Caronte,
> Tú libérame ya de sutileza,
> Madre y caudal de lágrima que empieza
> En mí y no para ni en el horizonte!
> — ¡Dame tú ceguedad con que yo afronte
> Rumbo infinible de vida y belleza! . . .
> ¡Y la mudez con que el eterno expresa! . . .
> ¡Y el mi cadáver la tu boza apronte!
> — ¡Más no discurra yo sobre la linfa,
> Ni rebusque ni finja, en haz o seno
> De insondable hora, nenúfar o ninfa!
> — ¡De los ojos del muerto, mi mirada
> Paire en faceta a luz cristalizada
> Y yo mire belleza así sereno!

In the first stanza death is represented by the figure of Charon who, in Greek mythology, ferries the dead across the river Styx to the underworld. Evoking the rhythm of the mythical boatman's stroke, Adán appeals to it to free him from the subtlety which has been the bane of his artistic career, the excessive intellectualism which has been a source of endless suffering to him since it is precisely his lack of emotional simplicity which has prevented him from apprehending through poetry the greater reality after which he hungers.

The second stanza is based on the paradox, already voiced in the epigraph by Fray Luis, that death is the source of true life. Absolute beauty, invisible to human eyes, and infinite harmony, inexpressible in human language, are located in the silent darkness beyond the grave. Hence the poet pleads to be stripped of his human faculties in death and to be endowed with the blindness with which to contemplate eternal beauty and the dumbness with which to express the silent ecstasy inspired by eternal harmony. So anxious is he to embark on this last voyage towards the infinite that he wishes his corpse to hasten the boatman by casting off for him.

The nautical metaphor reappears in the first tercet where he expresses his weariness with the artistic adventure which has him wandering over the waters, scouring the oceans for the beauty which, like the water-lily, manifests itself on the surface of the temporal world or, like the water-nymph, is concealed in the unfathomable depths of eternity beneath the temporal, a beauty which his poetry can only simulate since it is beyond his power as a mere human to reproduce it in his verse. He longs, therefore, for the world beyond the grave where, through the eyes of a dead man, his gaze, like a ship at rest on an ocean whose surface appears in the sunlight as smooth and dazzling as a precious stone, can linger in serene contemplation of absolute beauty.

Thus, despite his failure fully to achieve his poetic goals, Adán ends the volume on an optimistic note with a view of death reminiscent of Eguren. Such optimism, however, was to prove difficult to maintain and his subsequent work is marked by an increasingly anguished metaphysical uncertainty.[11]

11. For a general study of Adán's work, see John Kinsella, "The tragic and its consolation: a study of the work of Martín Adán", Diss. Liverpool, 1977.